TRAVERSING THE
PATHWAYS

LINDI MASTERS

Contents

Chapter 1
The Tree of Life

Two of the foundational things that I engage with are: the Tree of Life, or as it's called in Hebrew, *sefirot*, and the other is the cube. We must understand that the Jews actually kept the mysteries for us and we're delighted that they did because if they hadn't, we would have lost them. Yahweh is now beginning to release and reveal to us His mysteries and we're going to study the *sefirot* because it's incredibly important to know the spiritual points in the body. I actually discovered them by accident; my husband and I were psalmists and we travelled to various places teaching psalmody. One day, by chance, I saw a picture showing the spiritual points in the body and I realised that these points correlated with what we sang about in worship, for example:

- We lift our hands in the most holy place
- We lift up our hands as an evening sacrifice
- Lift up your head, oh you gates
- Come and bow before the Lord
- Out of my belly will flow rivers of living water

I realised that the above Scriptures correlated with the points in the body that I saw on that picture. We must remember that the Bible was written by the Jews, for the Jews and we are grafted in. *Isaiah 9:6* says, "… The government is on His shoulders," therefore we must understand what that means. *Chesed* and *Gevurah* sit on our shoulders, which translated means that Lovingkindness and Mercy, Justice and Judgment are the four pillars of Love. Ultimately, it means that He governs from the place of Love. By understanding the spiritual points in the body, what they're there for and what they do, it will become easier to operate within our bodies. For the last five years we have had teachings on the spirituality of the body and how to deal with our 'junk'. I believe we do this by learning about the points in the body, dealing with our junk, learning how to engage with the twenty-two living letters within the body which when joined with the ten points make up the thirty-two pathways of Wisdom. One of the points in our body is connected to breath. I find it interesting that COVID attacks the breath and the lungs but if you know how to breathe with *Alef*, and you know where it is situated, you can actually come to a place of healing.

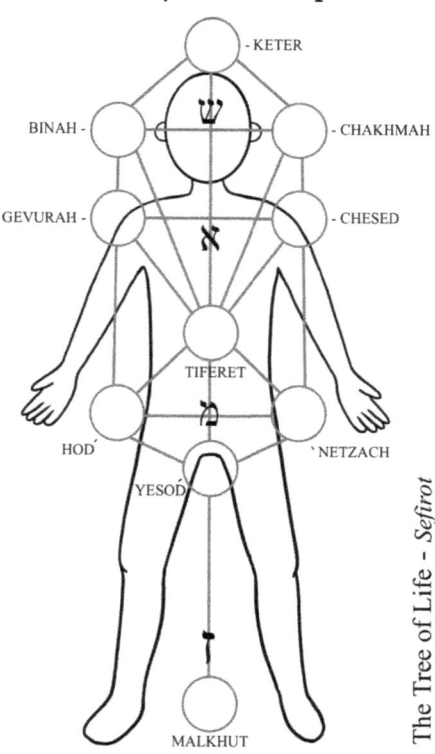

The Tree of Life - *Sefirot*

There are ten spiritual points in the body. The *Keter* is the head and the crown. Scripture says in *Psalm 24:7*, "Lift up your head oh ye gates, be lifted up, ye everlasting doors." We have often prayed that God would touch someone from the crown of their head to the soles of their feet. The *Keter* is a very strong ascension point in the body and when I worship I feel a burning sensation on my head as if something is pulling me through what I now understand is a gate.

When we look at this picture of the human form we view it from the back without inverting the right and left sides. On the right side is *Chakhmah* which is Wisdom and on the left side is *Binah* which is Understanding. When Yahweh speaks to me in an audible voice, I hear it in my right ear which is Wisdom speaking so that I can get understanding and knowledge. Knowledge is a secret point that is not added to the other ten points. It's a very powerful point called the *Da'at*, where all ten sefirot in the Tree of Life are united as one. *Chesed*, Lovingkindness, is on the right shoulder and *Gevurah*, Justice and Judgement, is on the left shoulder.

The *Tiferet*, or the belly, is referenced in *John 7:38* which says, "Out of your belly will flow rivers of living water." This is where the glory resides. Sometimes, when we feel a 'butterfly' sensation in our stomach, we say that the Holy Spirit is speaking when it is actually the glory beginning to be activated on the inside. It is also the seat of our emotion.

On the right hip is the *Netzach* which speaks about Victory and Endurance and on the left side is the *Hod* which is the Splendour and Awe of Yahweh. The *Yesod* sits between the belly button and reproductive organs and represents foundation, divine creativity and fertility. The *Malkhut* is very important because it is the connection between us and the earth. Scripture says in *Joshua 1:3*, "Every place that my foot shall tread, Yahweh has given to me."

Malkhut is like the *Vav* because it anchors or nails us into creation by using these pathways of glory and the pathways of the Tree of Life within us. *Matthew 6:9-10* says, "Our Father, Who Art in Heaven, hallowed be thy name, Your Kingdom come and Your will be done **on the earth** as it is in Heaven." This means we are a conduit of the Kingdom and all that Yahweh wants to release through us from the *Choshek*, through all of the pathways within us, into the face of the earth through the *Malkhut*.

Within you there is the Tree of Life. Those outside of Christ access the Tree of the Knowledge of Good and Evil. The *Shin* is placed on the forehead below the *Keter* in the Tree of Life, while the Third Eye is accessed through the Tree of the Knowledge of Good and Evil. The *Alef* is placed between *Chesed* and *Gevurah*, and the *Mem* between *Netzach* and *Hod*. These three living letters are called the Three Mothers. It's interesting that at the place where we lift up our head or gate, between Wisdom and Understanding, is the *Shin*, which places us within His name when we say, "*Yod Hey Shin Vav Hey*." The *Shin* also speaks about hooking into the things of the Kingdom.

The *Alef* is placed in the lung area. When we are breathing in and doing our meditation, we are automatically activating *Alef*, which is breath. When we say, "*Alef*," we say it with a 'breathy' sound which activates our lungs. Whether we are struggling with sickness or just want to have an activation on the inside, we need to learn how to activate and walk with *Alef* so that this letter can begin to work on the inside of who we are.

The *Mem* is the waters. Some of us remember our grandmothers saying, "Oh, my waters are off today!" The *Mem*, which sits between the hips has two parts; the upper waters and the lower waters which are depicted by the open *Mem* and the *Mem soffit*.

There is always a flowing from the upper waters into the lower waters. The Zohar says that the upper parts of God feed into the lower parts of God showing that He is an ever-moving horizon. Yahweh is not stagnant or static but always expanding. We're not going to get to Heaven, have knowledge of everything, and then get bored. I love that God is ever moving, ever expanding and that He's bigger than what we think He is.

The East Gate is where the glory enters into creation, and *Psalm 24:7-10* says, "Lift up your head oh ye gates, be lifted up the everlasting doors so the King of glory may come in. Who is this King of glory, the Lord strong and mighty? Who is this King of glory, the Lord mighty in battle?" East is actually at the *Keter*, West by the *Malkhut*, South is placed at *Chesed* and North at *Gevurah*. It's interesting to see where this places us with regards to the four points of the compass within our own bodies because East is always connected to the glory.

The days of creation are connected to the Tree of Life.
- *Chesed* (Lovingkindness) is connected to One Day (day one).
- *Gevurah* (Justice and Judgement) is connected to day two.
- *Tiferet* (glory and beauty) is connected to day three.
- *Netzach* (victory and endurance) is connected to day four.
- *Hod* (splendour and awe) is connected to day five.
- *Yesod* (creativity) is connected to day six.

Day seven is seated in the *Malkhut* which is the day God rested because He found a man to continue with what He had started. When Wisdom and Understanding arc within us, Knowledge presents itself. Pictures of the *Sefirot* show how all of the ten spiritual points in our body are connected to create the thirty-two pathways of Wisdom because every pathway has one of the Living Letters on it which, when activated, begin to work within us. As Christians, we were taught that this was demonic. I now go to a mystical therapist who practices reflexology whereas previously I used to tell people to repent if they had visited one themselves.

It is important, however, that the practitioner who is working on you is born from above and knows what they are doing. We have become so disconnected from our bodies and we don't want to dip into the things of the world instead of into the things of the Kingdom — the secrets are found in the Kingdom.

Aryeh Kaplan has written a book called the *Sefer Yetzirah*. The Jews don't have the blood of the Lamb but they do, up to a point, have the mysteries. This book also teaches you the intricate two-day process of how to create 'golems'. Scripture says in *Genesis 12:5*, "And Abram took Sarai his wife, and Lot his brother's son, and all their substance that they had gathered, and the souls that they had gotten in Haran; and they went forth to go into the land of Canaan; and into the land of Canaan they came." The phrase 'the souls that they had gotten' can also be read as: *the people they had made, acquired or fashioned.* That is a reference to the golems that Abraham was able to create. **Do not make golems** if you don't know what to do with them. They are genies in a bottle. Many things we read about in children's books or see in movies come from Jewish mysteries that have been hidden in plain sight.

The four pillars of Love are: Justice, Judgement, Grace and Mercy and when they arc they create what we call Love. Without Justice and Judgement there can be no Grace given to you or Mercy extended to you. This is why the hyper-grace doctrine is problematic. When we sin, we can go to the Courts, tell Yahweh what we have done and ask for judgment. In Scripture, justice and judgement are the same word. We then ask Him to forgive us and He gives us Grace and extends Mercy so that Love begins to work on the inside of us, releasing

Shekinah.

Scripture says that the government rests on His shoulders. What does that look like? When we look at the Tree of Life we see that *Chesed*, which is Lovingkindness (Grace and Mercy), rests on the right shoulder and *Gevurah*, which is Justice and Judgement, rests on the left shoulder.

This means that Love rests on His shoulders because the four pillars of Love are encompassed in the spiritual points on His shoulders. It's important for us to understand these points so that we can understand Scripture better. *Chesed* and *Gevurah* arc together to create Love.

The *Shekinah* (pronounced sh-KEEna) of Yahweh begins to be released in us when we're operating in the four pillars of Love. God does nothing unless He does it with *Shekinah*, on *Shekinah* and through *Shekinah*. This word isn't actually found in the Bible but it is part of our vernacular so we can understand that Yahweh always does everything with honour, through *Shekinah*. The Being of *Shekinah* has always been around Him and when she appears in our midst all sorts of crazy things start to happen. Scripture says in *Psalm 23:6*, "Surely Goodness and Mercy will follow me all the days of my life and I will dwell in the house of the Lord forever." Grace and Mercy are Beings. Goodness (Grace) is depicted as fire and is connected to Justice and Judgement while Mercy is equated to a cloud. We see evidence of Goodness (fire) and Mercy (cloud) in Scripture when we read about the Hebrews going through the waters and then into the wilderness. During the day they were followed by a pillar of cloud, (Mercy), and at night by a pillar of fire, (Goodness). When these two Beings arc they show the faces or *panaim* of Yahweh and *Shekinah* is released which takes us into the house of our God.

I didn't realise that Goodness and Mercy were beings until I had an encounter with them. In order to start a relationship with them all we need to do is turn towards Goodness and say, "Goodness, I want to know you. I honour you because I want to have a relationship with you."

Then we turn to Mercy and say the same thing. When I did that, I heard a voice in my ear telling me to look up a certain Scripture. When I read it, I found a name of Yahweh that I had never heard before. I spoke to a rabbi about it who told me that it was a secret name hidden by the Jews, and the only one who ever used it was Adam when he walked in the garden and spoke to Yahweh.

I heard that name because I had been introduced, through the pillars of Goodness and Mercy, into the faces or *panaim* of Yahweh which are His most intimate parts - the Lion, Ox, Eagle and Man. When He shows you His face, He's showing you everything that already was and everything that is going to come which is what Moses saw when he went up into the dark cloud. We think that Moses saw His back but he actually saw everything that had happened in the past as well as everything that was going to happen in the future, which is why he was able to write the five books of Moses. He wrote about the beginning, he wrote about his birth and he wrote about his death. We can have the same access.

The first time the faces of God are mentioned in Scripture is found in *Genesis 1:1-2*, "In the beginning God created the heavens and the earth." It's interesting that the word 'God' in verse 1 is *Elohim*, which is the plural form so we should be reading it like this: "In the beginning *gods* created the Heavens and the earth. The earth was without form, and void; and darkness was on the face of the deep. And the Spirit of God was hovering over the face of the waters." That darkness is the word *choshek* and it was on the faces or *panaim* of the deep.

The faces of the deep appeared to this Tribe — this mystical group — in 2018 when we were on a cruise in the Arctic Circle. While we were there, the circle of the deep, or compass of the deep mentioned in *Proverbs 8:27*, revealed itself and an angel, the keeper of the vaults of the deep, came out to meet us. They had not manifested themselves to mankind since *Genesis 1* and they asked, "Why have you brought these ones here?" The angel replied, "Because they are worthy." Since that encounter, they've been releasing mysteries from the vaults of the deep and South Africa in particular, experienced amazing restoration during a time period following that encounter with the faces of the deep.

During that cruise, our mandate was to restore some things at the North Gate which had been unlawfully opened, thereby allowing all kinds of unlawful things to be released. The only gate that stays open is the East Gate which is the gate that lets the glory come in. The other gates should not be touched yet. The time will come when we will be allowed to redeem the other gates.

The East should not be on the right side it should be above us which means that the earth, in its fourth estate, is facing the wrong way as a result of Lucifer's fall. Lucifer, Satan and the Great Dragon are three different Beings who all fell at around the same time. Lucifer was the star of the morning, Satan or ha-satan (written in lower case and always plural) refers to the irritations or the accusers of the brethren, and then there is the great dragon. They are the ungodly trinity while we have the Father, Son, and Holy Spirit.

With the North being situated at the top of the compass, some strange policies are being implemented in the world and the northern hemisphere is accessing things that are being rolled out on the face of the earth that have come from the morality of man. If these had come from the East, different policies would have been implemented. The magnetic North has moved more rapidly in the last few years than it has done in many years previously. It took decades for it to shift but now it's moving every month and is currently situated in Siberia. While I was in England, I had to use my GPS to assist me in getting to various destinations and for about two weeks, it would lead me to many arbitrary places. Technicians actually had to re-calibrate the satellites because there had been such a dramatic move of the magnetic North which gave out false directions.

We have four gates sitting on the face of the earth: North, South, East and West. Gates are not easy to open; it takes powerful people to open gates and powerful people to shut them. There was a man who had a group of people working with him, travelling around the world opening and shutting gates. I personally know people who have worked with him who have never fully recovered from the negative impacts of engaging with these gates. So, if I see a North gate, is it my job to do anything about it? Or, do I just acknowledge that I see it? Just because you can see something doesn't mean you have to do anything about it.

Someone once asked me why God was showing them things if they were not meant to act on it. I replied that I can see, so God doesn't have to show me things. Most of the time, it has nothing to do with us and those gates are not to be trifled with. The North, West and South gates are massive and they open into other realms which still need to be redeemed but Yahweh hasn't released us to do anything with them yet.

When we legislate, we must expect evidence. About a week after our encounter with the faces of the deep we heard a low sound vibrating through the building we were in. Soon after, an article was posted on the internet which reported that scientists had recorded a specific star in the southern hemisphere's planetary system that had moved and had started to draw a compass around another star. We had just seen the compass of the deep come out to meet us and shortly thereafter, one star had started drawing a compass around another star!

After we had seen the evidence of our engagement reflected in the cosmos, we heard that seismologists had picked up a strange vibration. It had started in the East and had travelled through Kenya making its way around the world. They could track it on their instruments and were waiting for the tremor to become an earthquake but nothing happened. They remarked that the tremor had a strange vibration – it was moving too fast. Both of those incidents happened within days of our encounter with the faces of the deep. We then knew we'd actually achieved something. We didn't close the gate but we did engage with the Beings that are around the gate so that we could begin to bring change on the face of the earth.

Our crown gate, the *Keter*, is always open and is an ascension point where we, as spirits, with our souls are able to go up and down. The easiest way for us to activate this point is through worship or praying in the Spirit. Our hands are also ascension points which is why palm readers can 'read' us.
If we extend our hands in front of us and concentrate on those ascension points, we can actually feel a vibration in the middle of our palms. In *Psalm 134:2* Scripture says that we must lift up our hands in the holy place and in *Psalm 141:2* it says our prayers are as incense before Him and the lifting up of our hands are as an evening sacrifice. We have not understood the doctrine of laying on of hands (*Hebrews 6:2*).
The ten spiritual points found in our body are also found in our ten fingers. The Hebrew word, *zamar*, which is translated

as 'praise' means to play or pick an instrument or used in the context of lifting up our hands to praise Him or used to show the touching of each finger to the thumb.

Sometimes, when the Jews worship, you will see them touching their thumbs to each of their fingers in turn and by doing that they are activating the ten gates found in both the body and the fingers.

One day, while I was listening to someone preach, I was touching my fingers with my thumbs. A Messianic Jew asked me why I did that and I told them that I had no idea. I didn't realise that I was doing *zamar*, or praising Him, by playing the instruments of my fingers.

Everything is connected. You also have the points of the Tree of Life in your feet. I have the tree of God, the Tree of Life in me, so when my feet touch the ground, I am releasing the fullness of that Tree from within my body, through me, into the face of the earth. When some of the watchers fell, they had children with the women on earth who produced the men of renown. These offspring had six fingers and six toes. These came from the false tree, not from the true tree.

The *Shin*, *Alef* and *Mem*, found in our head, chest and belly are also known as the Three Mothers. The *Shin* releases a hissing sound of 'sh' or 's' and is associated with fire and Binah or understanding. The *Mem*, which is found in the belly and is the receptive power, makes a humming sound and is very calm. It is associated with water. This is also the place of the still, small voice. In South Africa, we have an Afrikaans word, *omgekrap*, which means we feel uncomfortable or out of sorts. This is because the upper and lower waters haven't come to a place of spiritual balance so there is a sort of butterfly feeling within. How do you fix it? You speak in tongues or you meditate or you can even hum until you come to a place where the chaos is transformed into balance on the inside of you, through the *Tiferet*, and the *Mem* begins to hum.

Alef, which is between the *Keter* and the *Mem*, is breathe/air. *Alef* is both receptive and creative. When I breath in through my mouth, I begin to pull, from the *choshek*, into that gate and down into me where the *Alef* is represented. I hold that breath and when I release it out of my mouth I pull what I received from the *choshek* into my body. I can then either release it from my belly, the area from where rivers of living waters flow, or I can go right down into the *Yesod* and through my feet, *malkuth*, into the face of the earth. This is not hard even through it might sound complicated. Just keep practicing. If you lose your joy doing this, then you've lost everything. Just have fun!

We can also just step through the Blood of the Lamb, however, I do believe that it's beneficial for us to have an understanding of these spiritual points which are all linked to our physical body. If you suddenly have a ringing sound or an ache in your right ear it's generally because Wisdom is trying to say something to you but you're not listening, or, you might have heard something but you don't have the knowledge to understand it and so your thyroid starts to give problems.
If my right hip suddenly starts aching, then I look at victory and endurance and ask myself in which area am I not pushing through in victory? If it's my left hip, where the splendour of Yahweh is, then I look to see if I've lost the splendour, the awe and the beauty of His name.

One of the books I use is called **Releasing Emotional Patterns with Essential Oils** by Carolyn L. Mein, D.C. and is a great tool. She discusses our emotions, why they are there and where they sit in the body. Two days after my husband transitioned to glory I started coughing and didn't stop for about three years.

19

I didn't know that grief is stored in the lungs and until I had dealt with the grief in the lungs, the coughing didn't stop. I once had a pain in my liver and found out that we store hate in that organ. I'm not an angry person by nature but I was angry with something that was an unjust issue and I had allowed that hate to lodge itself in my liver. In order to fix this, I started using oils on that area and I repented to my liver as well as doing a liver cleanse. I also changed my diet, all the while speaking to that organ. Sometimes, if we feel lonely, and we don't feel connected with those that are around us, then the way to get out of this loneliness is to find a loving place in Yahweh or with people. The organ that feels loneliness is the heart. Hope deferred makes the heart sick.

The author of the book works through the parts of the body and explains which emotions trigger the relevant body part. When we start learning that our body is phenomenal and that it's beautifully made, we realise that it is a temple which is as divine as us as spirits and our souls. When we understand that, we can start listening to our body.

I've started doing what is called muscle testing. I love working with all these points in my body because I'm learning how to bring my body into divinity. It's so divine that Yahweh has let the Holy Spirit live in it! The Church on the other hand teaches us how to beat up our body because it is sinful and *Romans 7:8* says there is no good thing in the flesh. I'm not talking about getting my body into shape at gym but rather how divine it is. I'll choose an oil, stand with my feet together, close my eyes, hold the oil against my heart and I ask my body whether I need this oil today. If I need it, my body moves forward. If I don't need it, my body moves backwards. You can't really fabricate this; it just does what it has to do.

When I came back to South Africa, I was really exhausted. I'd been travelling extensively, visiting all twenty-five hubs in England every month, and I was tired. While I was in South Africa, we went into lockdown and my whole endocrinal system shut down. I couldn't travel anywhere so I had to learn to listen to my body. I had to apologise and repent to it and I had to rebuild it to a place of wholeness. I'm grateful for lockdown because I was able to deal with the issue at hand.

A friend has been teaching me about buying crockery as an investment. My portfolio consists of gold, silver, finances, investments and various pieces of crockery that have gold or silver leaf on them. I found a particular silver-plated piece from Yugoslavia as well as a pewter sugar bowl.

While I was in the store I picked both up and wondered which one I should buy. I held the sugar bowl against my chest and asked my body if I needed to buy it. In response, my body went backwards. I then did the same with the piece of crockery and my body responded by moving forward, so I bought it. When I got home with my purchase I inspected it and saw by the markings on the bottom that I had gotten myself a real bargain. The piece was out of production and therefore, highly sought after.

Because of the divinity of my body, I love looking at how the different spiritual points are reflected through the *Malkhut* into the face of the earth. The ten spiritual points and the twenty-two Living Letters which make up the thirty-two pathways of Wisdom are activated by praying in the spirit and embed the secrets of Yahweh into your DNA. Once activated, the pathways move through the spiritual points in your body including the *Yesod*, the creative part of who you are.

The Greek word, *mystirio*, comes from another Greek word, *muo*, which means to be closed or to shut. We can therefore hold the mysteries in the *Yesod* without necessarily speaking. When we pray in the Spirit and hold the mysteries in the *Yesod*, at some point the *Ruach* will let you know that you can release them through the *Malkhut*, represented in your feet, which are grounded on the face of the earth.

We've all seen pictures which depict the outline of a human form that has lines going through various points forming triangles and cubes. A lot of these drawings are done by New Agers who get this information from the Tree of the Knowledge of Good and Evil which is all found below the sun. When I look at that picture I can see my DNA running through my body as the mysteries begin to be activated on the inside of me. We have access to two other letters that were hidden from humanity: The *Shin Gadol*, which was hidden in the *Shin*, and the *Ghah*, which was hidden in the *Ayin*.

These two letters are known as ascension letters. The Jews hid them so that people could not find them and misuse them. When I reach up into the *choshek*, through the points in my body, I go through that door and into the secrets of Yahweh. *Proverbs 25:2* says that the secrets of Yahweh are only for those who seek them out. These mysteries are found in the *choshek* but the secrets sit in the dark cloud of the Lord. The Jews were given the right to protect what was in the *choshek*.
Moses went into the dark cloud of the Lord and began to see the secrets of Yahweh. The Jews have held the secrets in the upper waters and the mysteries in the lower waters of Yahweh. When we pray in the Spirit we should hold the mysteries in silence in the secret place within us.

Interestingly, scientists have named a particular section within our DNA the 'God particle'. When I pray, I reach up through the *Ghah*, and I begin to go up into the secrets of Yahweh so that

I can 'fish' in the *choshek*. The priests would use a hook shaped like the *Shin* and they would throw it into the pot of the daily meat sacrifice. Whatever was pulled out of the pot was their 'daily bread.' That is found in one of our prayers: "Give us this day our daily bread."

The priests received their daily portion; not too much and not too little. This is not only referring to our daily supply but it's also about being able reach in and getting our secrets for the day and then coming back down through our spiritual points. We then hold them in the *Yesod*, which holds the mysteries within us, until the Holy Spirit says we can release them onto the face of the earth because the whole of creation is groaning and waiting for the manifestation of the sons to bring the earth back into its original estate. This is found in *Romans 8:22*. When we bow before the Lord, it's one of the easiest places, as a spirit, for our souls to rise up into the realms of the Kingdom. Bowing isn't to make us feel subservient because we're His sons who are made a little lower than *Elohim*, not a little lower than angels. I've been bowing down for many years and this ascension point in my body is now open.

A friend of mine had a problem with his liver. When he went for a check-up, his Jewish doctor told him that the People of the Way didn't know how to look after their body when they slept at night. He also said that the liver and kidneys are the organs that can 'see' and many Christians have issues within these parts of the body. He explained that Jews pray over their body so that when it's in rest, they, as a spirit with a soul, can do what they have to do in the Kingdom realms. When they wake up in the morning they come back into the body. Many times, we wake up and say that we had the strangest dream.

We didn't actually have a dream – we had an encounter.

We need to reframe this and call them dream encounters, because we as spirits, with our soul, have been busy elsewhere. Sometimes we don't know how to frame what we've seen so if we had a dream of a ship sailing on an ocean, and a big wave came and then a whale popped up we'll just call it a strange dream. A ship can mean a ministry, and the ocean can represent people while a whale could be a star system. Yahweh is speaking to us but because we don't know how to frame what we see we turn to dream interpretation books to try and help us to untangle what we have been doing.

There are angels stationed 'around the clock' from six to nine, nine to twelve, twelve to three and three to six. They guard the hours in your night watch. We now understand, that in Jewish thinking, night time is not the end of the day. Their day starts at sun down and goes through to the following sun down while our day starts in the morning and finishes at night. Your day actually starts when you go to bed at night. The secrets are to be found in the *choshek*, in the darkness, so when you go to sleep, you're going to sleep in the mysteries. As a spirit and soul you engage with what you need to do so that when you wake up in the morning the angel stationed at six o'clock will read out, into the gate of the morning, all that you have engaged with through the night watches so that it can order your day and you can walk out all of those mysteries as a star of the morning.

We need to know how to bring our bodies into a place of rest. Rest is not the absence of being busy nor is it the absence of terror but it's knowing how to bring your body into a place of rest, regardless of what's going on around you. I bring my body to rest by breathing exercises, saying the *Yod Hey Vav Hey*, speaking in tongues and praying in the Spirit and going through my meditation. These all help me to find a place of rest and peace within my body. David would talk to his soul and ask it why it was disquieted within him, *Psalm 42:5*.

I believe that Adam originally looked like a spiritual light-being with DNA travelling up and down and all the pathways of Wisdom running through him. He had the menorah, the golden bowl and the wheel within a wheel, that was full of eyes, sitting within him as well. As a spirit being, he operated between heaven and earth, going in and out, walking in the garden with Yahweh.

As a result of being overshadowed by the wrong tree and being sent out of the garden, God had to put skin on him – not an animal skin - this is where his soul and spirit went inward and his body came to be on the outside. We need to become aware of the fact that we are light-beings which is why it's important for us to bring our bodies to a place of divinity, *John 12:36*. The Church has taught us that there's no good thing in the flesh, that all our problems are in the soul and the only thing of real importance is our spirit. This is all a lie. Jasher records in his book that Nimrod took Adam's skin and put it on. The skin was later passed down generationally because they knew that there was something spectacular and divine about the body. We must be careful not to superimpose our 21st century thinking onto this practice because not too long ago, the Egyptians were mummifying people.

After I was born again from above, I still had the same body. As a spirit, I came alive and wasn't dormant anymore because the silver cord was destroyed and the golden bowl was lit and I was born again. We see this is *2 Corinthians 5:17*. My soul had become new, my body remained the same and my spirit cannot die. Two weeks later I was still dealing with the same old junk from before I was saved. I had felt rejected before I was saved and I still felt rejected after I was saved. I believe that it is not your soul that is the issue; it is the cellular memory that sits in your DNA that is the issue. It's the memory of your parents and your grandparents and all the others that came before them which are within you, reminding you of the past.

This is fantastic news for us, because we are then able to deal with the corrupted parts within our DNA. My soul had become a new creature and as a spirit-being, I was awake. I could now bring my body into a place of divinity because the Holy Spirit had come to live in it. I'm a temple. So, my issue was actually cellular memory which means I had to deal with my DNA. When I saw my DNA coming out of my belly, looking like a twirling ladder, I knew I had to deal with my junk. I had absolutely no idea what that meant! I eventually figured it out and started to deal with it while I was on a long road trip. I saw my DNA going up and I started to go up with it in thought speed. I saw a trading floor and I realized it was a trading floor that my ancestors had traded into for power that was causing me trouble. I had suffered from upper backache because of a Jezebel spirit in my family line so I had to deal with that.

In many of these instances we have to go to the Mobile Court first, which is where we get the papers so that we can repent and ask God for judgement to be meted out so that we can legally deal into the trading floors. Many of the things we are looking for are hiding in plain sight in order to keep the mysteries alive. Let's look at some children's stories:

  - Jack buys some beans, throws them on the ground and overnight they grow into a huge beanstalk. At the top lives a giant who has stolen the golden egg so Jack has to climb up the beanstalk to get back his inheritance. This story mirrors what we are dealing with.
  - Abracadabra is a Hebrew word which means 'the thing that I speak I can create.'

- Aladdin rides on a flying carpet which is the dias that we can travel on.

- Hey Diddle Diddle, the cat and the fiddle, the cow jumped over the moon. How does a cow jump over the moon? The cow is actually Taurus jumping over the moon so he can bring the *Mazzaroth* back into its original intent because when Lucifer fell, he corrupted the *Mazzaroth* and it became the zodiac which is 12.5 degrees off it's proper tilt. The 'cow' jumping over the moon is bringing it back to its original intent.

- What do you think hopscotch is? It's the *sefirot* - The Tree of Life.

Everything is in plain sight except that we don't know it's there. I'm a big Marvel fan and in one of the latest Marvel movies, Thanos has a glove encrusted with gem stones and wants to get rid of the earth. That glove is the exact replica of the one that the priests put the hand of Teresa of Avila into after she had died. Franco of Spain knew that there was something very powerful about that relic so he stole it and he had it near him at all times because he said it helped him to be powerful. When he fell ill, his bed was placed near that glove because of the power attached to it.

Looking at all these stories we see that there is nothing new under the sun. These are the mysteries that the Jews kept which Yahweh is now giving us an opportunity to discover. This is not difficult; it's a great and wonderful journey.

Chapter 2
The Menorah Within

The cube, the Tree of Life or the echo chamber can be complicated subjects but we should not walk away from something just because we don't understand it. When we stand within the name of Yahweh and we speak out the *Yod Hey Vav Hey*, we are creating an echo chamber around us — it's not just a 'flat' word — we become the echo of His name, creating a vortex of Living Letters around ourselves.

Yahweh's only command to first creation man was to be fruitful, to multiply, and to replenish. How do we replenish? The only way we can do this is to copy the way He did it, by using the Living Letters and forming them into different combinations to create sounds and words. That is how the physical world was created. The name of Yahweh within us starts to echo outwards and creation always responds to the echo of His name, whether we say it out loud or not. Within us, the thirty-two pathways of Wisdom, including the twenty-two letters, are always echoing. This is not new revelation; we've always known this and done this, but we didn't have a framework or language for it. We need to understand the theology behind why we say the *Yod Hey Vav Hey*.

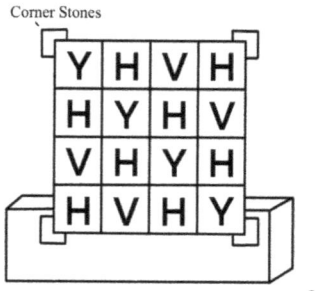

Corner Stones

Y	H	V	H
H	Y	H	V
V	H	Y	H
H	V	H	Y

The Echo Chamber

28

I had an encounter once where I was literally standing next to my body, which was asleep in my bed, saying, "Come on, wake up, wake up! We need to do this!"

When I woke up, I thought how weird that was but the following night the same thing happened. I, as a spirit and soul, was standing next to my body, looking at it, willing it to wake up and realizing that this was not a dream but an encounter. Our body rests in bed and may sometimes trans-relocate, but mostly it rests while we as spirit-beings with our souls go back to Zion, into the realms of the Kingdom, regardless of whether we are aware of it or not. We encounter things in the terrestrial or celestial realm which we then say is déjà vu, dreams or visions.

To use an example — there's going to be volcanic activity and in 'old school Christianity', the way I used to talk, I will say that I'm feeling uneasy in my spirit and I start to speak in tongues. I do believe that Holy Spirit is involved in this process but I also believe that I'm quantumly entangled and so my terrestrial body sees that there is going to be an earthquake and calls me, saying, "Lindi, there's going to be an earthquake," and my natural body turns to look.

In the 'old speak', I would have said that Holy Spirit is warning me or that my spirit had discerned something. I am now framing it in a new language and training myself to realize that when I'm feeling something, I must turn my attention to which one of my bodies is calling me from the Kingdom realm so that I pray in the Spirit and engage and arc with that body. I believe we have encounters every night but we haven't trained ourselves to remember them. We can however, dream silly things, especially if our body needs to work hard at digesting a large meal. Many dream books have been written because people don't know how to interpret their own dreams. When we dream about some kind of transport, it's usually referring to our ministry but because we haven't trained ourselves yet to see our ministry taking a turn in another direction, we will dream that a vehicle of some sort is traveling and turning which we then interpret through a filter.

Kabbalah is the practice of studying the mysteries of Yahweh through the mystical interpretation of Scripture. There are three separate streams of Kabbalah but most of us were not aware of its existence until Madonna popularized it.

- The branch of Kabbalah which involves the occult is satanic in nature and involves dark magic practices which we don't engage with.
- The branch of Kabbalah that Madonna made popular uses the 72 names of Yahweh to access the mysteries in order to bring oneself into a place of divine consciousness by trying to reach God, whom they do not know. This is almost like building a tower of Babel. We also don't involve ourselves in this form of Kabbalah.
- The third type of Kabbalah is what Yeshua, as a high priest, would have practiced — the ancient Jewish tradition of mystical interpretation of the Tanakh.

The written mysteries were kept in secret by the Jews but Yahweh has now removed the veil and we are able to access these same secrets of Yahweh because of the blood of the Lamb. We don't have to activate points on our body to enter the realms of the Kingdom — we can just breathe and we're in front of Him and with Him. Even so, many of us do engage with the Tree of Life and I feel it's important for us to know how it presents itself in our body and how connected we are to the Living Letters and to the whole of creation within us.

I've had some of the Living Letters appear to me, with *Ayin* being a particularly important letter who materialized in a room full of people which was captured in a photo. I love all the letters but I favour the *Mem*. Generally, it's a really holy moment when they engage with me, almost like a holy fear.

The letters are holy and part of who Yahweh is. At the moment, I'm engaging with the *Ghah* and the *Shin Gadol* which have only been introduced to us in the last ten years or so as they have been in hiddenness. They are two very powerful ascension letters and were kept hidden by the Jews on purpose so the Gentiles and the pagans couldn't find them and abuse their power.

I do struggle a little when I see Christians publicly wearing these two letters in the form of jewellery or printed on clothing; these letters were kept in secrecy by the Jews and the Essenes. On one occasion, I was flying to Los Angeles and was wearing a shirt that had the *Yod Hey Shin Vav Hey* on it which we had printed for one of our Intensive Conferences. Holy Spirit told me as clear as a bell not to wear that shirt on the plane so I quickly changed into something else. When I boarded, I was seated in a section made up of mostly Hasidic Jewish men! They would have gladly thrown me out of the plane. I was so grateful that I had listened to Holy Spirit because it would have been incredibly inappropriate to wear those names in public.

When I was still involved in the Church Age, I would scoff at the idea that people saw their dead relatives because I believed them to be demons. I've now discovered that those who have died and have gone on before us do still have assignments with us and are part of the cloud of witnesses.

The Men in White Linen around your own life could be one of your grandparents or great-grandparents and also include the patriarchs like Abraham, Isaac and Jacob and also the matriarchs of old. They are called that because of the long white robes that they wear. Many times, when someone is on their deathbed; they may see a dead relative in the room. I also engage with a few of the Prince Warring Angels and the Seraphim as well as the Watchers. I've had encounters with Watchers in various places and I engaged with them when there were some political changes taking place in South Africa. The Watchers are different Beings to the Watcher Giants. The Men of Renown have a bad reputation but can be redeemed while Beings like Metatron actually pre-date the book of Genesis. It was Metatron who created the pathways for Enoch, who was human, to walk on. I've also had an interesting time learning how to walk with Melchizedek.

Since my husband went to glory a number of years ago, I've seen him on different occasions. I've also seen my mother and my daughter-in-law's mom who had both transitioned. When my youngest son decided it was time to get married, a friend agreed to come and do the wedding ceremony. The weather man predicted a marvellously sunny day but the weather changed and the clouds started racing overhead. Big raindrops began to fall but fortunately didn't last very long. While we were drying the chairs the lightning was streaking across the sky. When my brother and I started engaging and reminding Yahweh that we were busy with an outdoor wedding, the lightning eased a little but the clouds were still racing. When we took the bridal couple's hands to pray a blessing over them a lightning bolt cracked right beside us on the other side of the fence and then the sun appeared as if nothing had happened. My friend turned to look at me and asked me if I had seen 'him'. I replied that I had been too busy making sure that all the guests were still accounted for! He then said that he had seen Ron, my husband, coming on a lightning bolt to oversee his son's wedding. My husband still has a massive mandate over that particular child and also over my grandchildren. My granddaughter has told us that her Grandpa Ron comes to see her in the house all the time which goes to show that he still has a mandate with his heritage.

When I've mentioned that I've had encounters people ask me to tell them what happened. I'm allowed to say who I encountered but I haven't been given permission to always share what happened in those encounters because they are for me personally and are not to be shared with everyone. Sometimes, I feel a little grieved when I see young mystics, who have come out of hiddenness, reveal everything on social media for the public to devour. I believe the depth of their encounters will diminish because people don't know how to '*muo*' or be quiet. There will come a time for these mysteries to be released, we just mustn't release them too early. The Essenes wrote the mysteries down and kept them in secret. According to the book of Jasher, Enoch had trained up about 70 of the Essenes and they ascended with him. They exchanged this world for that world and gave up their family here to go there. They kept it in mystery and I think we should too.

I had an encounter with *haDerech*, The Way, in which the whole path stood up and looked at me. It then told me that I could call it The Way. Lining the sides of the pathway were Essenes. They were clapping and handing us documents which contained the secrets. I could see by the expression on their faces that they were asking us to hold the secrets as honourably as they had done. Yahweh speaks in mystery and when I got saved at 17 I used to wonder why Jesus always spoke in parables and why He didn't just say what He meant. It seems to be the way of Yahweh that He hides things so that we have to seek them out; *Proverbs 25:2* – It is the *Kavod Elohim* to conceal a thing, but the *kavod melachim* is to search out a matter.

There is much spiritual information available on the internet but it comes from the Tree of the Knowledge of Good and Evil. These practitioners have understood the truth which lies within, while Christians have called it new age and demonic. One of the reasons I like to engage with the *Sefirot*, the godly Tree of Life, and with the cube, is because we can bring it to its rightful place within us and we can change the world and creation. The Jews have a seven branched candlestick which is hidden in mystery, called the menorah, and it is actually embedded within us. We must remember that the mysteries are always in plain sight because there must always be a record of them on the face of the earth. Gentiles may see a candelabra while the Jews know it's alluding to the Tree of Life. When the mystical Jewish men pray, they wear a little box called a phylactery tied to their forehead. The front of the box displays the *Shin* and the back of the box displays the *Shin Gadol*. The mystics know that the *Shin Gadol* can be used as an ascension point.

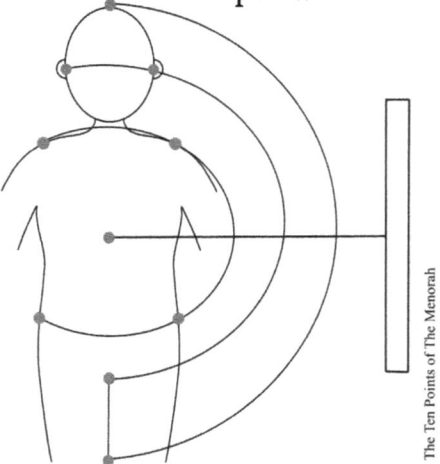

The Ten Points of The Menorah

Before Yahweh created anything, He communicated in a Heavenly language that we call tongues; He didn't just use cardiognosis or thoughts. When He said, "Let there be...."

He created the Living Letters and placed them in different combinations to create sound, action and formation which is when they became a language. In earthly languages, we combine different letters to create phonic sounds but they do not have the same power to create as the Living Letters do. When Yahweh spoke, the Letters came together in different formations to create what He said.

Now, because of the blood of the Lamb and because of who we are, those same letters present themselves within us when we speak in tongues and say the *Yod Hey Vav Hey*. If Yahweh did this to create, then it stands to reason that the ability to create sits within us too because we are using those same Letters. Scripture tells us that we can call those things that are not, as though they are *Romans 4:17*.

As good charismatic Christians, we would call things into being 'in Jesus' name,' when in fact, just by speaking in tongues and engaging with the Kingdom within, you and I can start to bring change on the face of the earth and to creation. Creation automatically responds to you just because of what flows through your body. In *Luke 17:20-21* Scripture says, 'Now when He was asked by the Pharisees when the kingdom of God would come, He answered them and said, "The kingdom of God does not come with observation; nor will they say, 'See here!' or 'See there!' For indeed, the kingdom of God is within you." Our understanding of Scripture is mostly very basic and shallow; Yeshua was trained up in what, today, we would call Kabbalah or the mysteries and secrets. A Jew who understands the *Sefirot* will know exactly what He meant by that statement in Luke.

What does it actually mean to have the Kingdom of Heaven within us and what does that look like?
I never doubted that fact and just accepted it as part of my life without really understanding it. When we look at a

drawing of what the basic *Sefirot*, or Tree of Life, looks like within the outline of a body we see the Crown; Wisdom and Understanding; Lovingkindness and Mercy. Out of our belly flows the glory, or the living waters; Victory and Endurance; Splendour and Awe. The *Yesod* houses Creativity and creation while *Zayin* is connected to the *Tiferet* which is connected to the *Yesod* and anchored into the face of the earth. The Kingdom of God within us is like the seven-branched Menorah lying on its side within our body with the seven points connecting to the gates which can be accessed once we are born from above. The glory is always in the middle of the Menorah which is where the golden bowl sits. This bowl never runs dry and feeds everything inside of us. I've actually seen the menorah embedded within me - it's not one-sided - because in Jewish understanding nothing is linear, it's always circular which means that there is a menorah on both sides, creating a wheel within a wheel within a wheel, which are all turning and spinning within us. If we look at the menorah within us, everywhere that has the rings crossing over with the other rings is a point which forms a gate. There are thirteen gates on the inside of us when the two menorahs are placed together and the Kingdom realms can then be explored.

In *2 Corinthians 12:2,* Paul wrote about his encounter when he went up to the third heaven. To help us understand what it means to have the Kingdom of Heaven within us we need to look at the seven different realms of the Kingdom.

Let's start with the first branch of the Menorah, (when we look at this we must remember that it's lying on its side) which is the Kingdom of the earth.
The second branch is the Kingdom of God.
The third branch is the Kingdom of Heaven.
The fourth one, the main one in the middle, is Heaven.

The fifth one is the Heaven of Heavens.
The sixth one is Perfection.
The seventh is Eternity.

Throughout the centuries, mystics have had encounters with these realms which they recorded in ancient texts. Although allusions to these Kingdoms can be found within the Bible, they are hidden. The sideways Menorah within us depicts the seven main realms of Heaven while on the end of each arm of the Menorah we find another Menorah. Through calculations, we can deduce that there are at least forty-nine different realms of the Kingdom, which means that there is not just one Heaven.

Paul's third Heaven encounter was in the Kingdom of Heaven which was on the third arm of the Menorah within himself which is why Scripture says that the Kingdom of Heaven is **within** us. The third letter of the Aleph Bet is *Gimel*, or the camel, which runs to the *Dalet* and is depicted by a foot. It also means 'full supply.' What Paul was really saying in that Scripture was that he went to the Kingdom of Heaven, the place of full supply. It was written in mystery!

Scripture speaks about the eyes around the throne of Yahweh. These eyes are called Ophenim. I've been to the throne of Yahweh and I remember looking at the rainbow which sits over His throne and I noticed eyes everywhere. They were blinking at me! These same eyes are also positioned within us on the Menorah.

The veil is on one side of the Menorah with the blood of the Lamb on the other picturing the old and the new covenant. In *Hebrews 10:19-21* we read, "Therefore, brethren, having boldness to enter the Holiest by the blood of Jesus, by a new and living way which He consecrated for us, through the veil, that is, His flesh, and having a High Priest over the house of God," and *Luke 22:20* says, Likewise He also took the cup after supper, saying, "This cup is the new covenant in My blood, which is shed for you."

The Court structure, made up of ten Courts, is also found within the Menorah. One of the Courts is called the Mobile Court because it can move anywhere and at any time and anyone has access to this, where one can judge anything that is accusing us. The accuser of the brethren can only access the Mobile Court because Scripture says he stands at our right hand to accuse us. Our bookstores are full of literature describing the demonic which is under the sun. We must go to the Mobile Court so we can deal with anything that hasatan is accusing us of. We now have boldness to step through and enter in by the blood of the Lamb so we can ascend, within ourselves, into the realms of the Kingdom.

The seven Spirits of Yahweh operate from the Courts and are there to teach us. These seven Spirits each have a colour and a function. The *Shin*, *Alef* and *Mem*, the three Mothers, are also within us, along with all the other Living Letters. Each letter has an angel as well as a colour, number and frequency. All of this sits within us, because Scripture says that the Kingdom of God is within us.

Scripture says that the government sits on His shoulders. We know that Love is made up of the four pillars of Lovingkindness, Mercy, Justice and Judgement. When they are combined they form the cube within us. Everything within us goes through our *Malkhut* and into creation and the whole of creation is groaning and waiting for the manifestation of the sons. The Church has been taught that we're going to be raptured, yet this is the truth of what sits on the inside of us.

Why would we want to be taken away when all of creation is groaning and waiting for us to be made manifest?

When I'm engaging, saying the *Yod Hey Vav Hey* and praying in the Spirit, I sometimes reach my hands up into the *Choshek* because I'm trying to create a mental and physical pathway for my body to feel me do the action. When looking at the picture of the body we can see where the upper waters and the lower waters come together in the *Tiferet*. This is the place where the waters are brought together to bring peace, stability and calmness within us. It's the place where chaos is brought into balance.

We have something called the Matrix of Fire running through us. When Elijah was taken up into heaven, the Jews recognized that it was the Living Letter, *Ghah*, that Elijah had connected with. Christians talk about a whirlwind taking Elijah up in a chariot. The chariot was actually a living Being and the whirlwind was the Letter *Ghah*. The *Shin Gadol* is also part of the ascension letters and is represented by fire. These two Letters are wind and fire. As we engage, through the spiritual points in our body, our DNA strands start ascending and descending and we are able to ascend into the *Choshek* to bring the mysteries and secrets back down again through our body. By doing this we are reaching through the Matrix of Fire, into the *Choshek*, the dark cloud of the Lord, and we take our daily supply by pulling it back through our body and into the face of the earth. We do this because creation is groaning and waiting for us to manifest ourselves.

Scripture says that God put skins on Adam after he ate from the wrong tree. Thanks to Constantine and King James we were taught that an animal was killed so that its skin could be used to clothe him. The Book of Jasher records that when Adam died everybody from every part of the earth was called together because the father of mankind had died. His skins were passed down through the generations until Nimrod came in possession of them. He put them on and began to be a powerful hunter before the Lord. Before Yahweh clothed Adam with skin, he was a white pulsating light.

When Yahweh said, "Let there be light," He was creating by using words formed by different combinations of the Living Letters. He then said to Adam that He was going to give him the animals to name. He didn't give Adam named animals, He told Adam to name them so Adam used the Hebrew Living Letters and created by stringing them together. When Yahweh presented Adam with an animal, Adam breathed life into it and named it. Yahweh then said, "Be fruitful and multiply and replenish." Replenish means 'to make more of something.' This same ability sits within us all.

When we start manifesting the fullness of Yahweh, we will look like Adam did while he was in the garden, as a spirit on the outside and our soul and body on the inside. When we lift up our hands, in worship to Yahweh, we are taking part in the evening sacrifice or the last sacrifice of the day which took place at 3pm. This was also the time that Yeshua gave up His Spirit on the cross. He said, "It is finished," and the final sacrifice was done; *John 19:30*. The lifting up of our hands in worship is the same thing as Yeshua on the cross because He begins to speak to us and we bring that communion back down, through our body. As we do this, creation starts to turn its attention towards us because we've begun to release the fullness of the Kingdom within us and the seven Spirits of Yahweh, with their seven colours and seven functions, also begin to operate from within us.

I have a very organic relationship with Yahweh. For many years I beat myself up for not being able to stick to a certain routine or read my Bible through in a year. I found it totally boring and even though I was the Pastor, I hated it! There is a saying that says, "A family that prays together, stays together."

My husband and I had very different sleep patterns; he would get up at 5am every morning to pray while I liked to sleep in but then I used to stay up late at night while he needed to go to bed. Needless to say, we hardly ever prayed together. Once, I got up at the same time as him but I brought my pillow with me. I woke up two hours later and had missed the whole thing. For a long while, I felt guilty for not having a regular routine with Yahweh. Over time, however, I've become very aware of all the spiritual points within me because I meditate on them so often. As a result, I'm in constant communion with Yahweh so if I need to engage for something, I will consciously engage with the different points in my body, reach into the *Choshek*, concentrate on meditation and breath work and then bring it down into my body. Speaking in tongues is important because it activates this whole process. This has nothing to do with works and everything to do with knowing who I am, sitting in my seat of rest.

I know that I've activated this within me because creation has begun to respond to me. My neighbour's trees grow over and under our dividing fence to come into my yard. My mom used to think it was crazy how all those trees and bushes looked like they wanted to be on our side of the fence. Why was that? My husband was a psalmist and we were always worshipping Yahweh and engaging with Him so we didn't have to make a set time to be in touch with Him. As a result, creation began to respond to us. My adult children always know when I'm about to arrive at the airport because the weather will suddenly shift. Once, a group of us engaged for a country that was in dire need of rain and broke that drought. I know what I carry and I know what I need to do.

One time I was in my home country with Ian Clayton and we were engaging with some of the Watchers. There were also three pyramids there and some stones that looked like Stonehenge. We were on a mountainside and our guide, Enosh from Swaziland, had wandered off to talk to the ancestors when the wind started blowing like crazy. I knew that we had definitely touched on something there. All of a sudden, Ian was overcome with emotion while he was engaging with the Watchers because he could hear then crying and weeping. They said that they had walked with mankind but had to leave the planet because Lucifer and the hordes that he had deceived and who had traded with him started to war against the Watchers on the face of the earth. The Watchers took their women and children, which is recorded in *Genesis 6:1-4*, and left the planet to watch over mankind. Archaeologists have found bones and skeletons of 30 foot giants.

We were talking to the good Watchers; we've always referred to them as the Nephilim. Some were good and some were bad. Those that fell were called the Men of Renown and were between 10 to 15-foot-tall, also known as the Goliath people. That area also has some ancient diamond mines and it has been said that Enoch walked among these very same mines. We know that wherever there is pressure in the earth, oil, coal or diamonds are to be found. Also, when a portal has touched the face of the earth, a diamond mine will be at that spot.

That night we stayed at a very smart farmhouse. Once the sun had set it was pitch dark outside and we couldn't see our hand in front of our face. I went to sleep and woke up at about 2am with light shining in my bedroom. Enoch was standing in my room along with other Ancient Ones and he was smiling at me. I was in a total panic and blurted out that he had come to the wrong room; Ian Clayton was in the next room. The next morning Ian asked if I had slept well so I told him about my encounter and that I had sent Enoch to his room!

The first time Ian came to stay at my home, I had only known him for a few days. We were going on a long road trip the next day and I was going to be driving one of the vehicles so I wanted to get a good night's rest. In the middle of the night there was so much talking going on in the passage outside my room that I eventually got up to ask them to tone it down a bit but when I opened the bedroom door, the passage was empty. I went to lay down again and the talking continued.
I got up to open the door again but there was nobody there. This time I lay down and just listened. I could hear people talking and doors opening and shutting. Then I heard, "Get behind me, I was here first." "No, YOU get behind me because I was here first." By this time, it was 4 o'clock in the morning. When I got up at 6 a.m. I was totally exhausted.

When I asked him how he had slept, he replied, "Oh, it was a busy night," to which I said, "Yes, I KNOW it was busy!" He apologized and said that he had told them to be quiet. That was my introduction to Ian's crazy life. At that stage, a rain cloud followed us everywhere we went. We could see what looked like a door in the cloud and for two weeks Ian would sit and engage with it and speak to it. It was really strange. However, at that point I knew that I had found my tribe and that I was going to stay around that man because I liked what he carried.
I've visited the place where the Book of Kells is housed. This book was written in about 300 A.D which makes it the oldest book in Ireland. It contains the gospels of Matthew, Mark, Luke and John, beautifully written on cow skin and it has the most amazing colours. It also depicts the Lion, Ox, Eagle and Man. They explain that Matthew was the Lion and Mark was the Eagle. They were so close to the truth but didn't get it quite right

because the Church didn't understand the mysteries.

That same university has a library containing 200,000 ancient books and as this is a working library you are allowed to go and find the secrets and mysteries that have been written down. Celtic art is full of patterns and lines intersecting each other. Often, there will be a pattern which depicts a wheel within a wheel which is completely Jewish in nature.

It was interesting to see that the Lion, Ox, Eagle and Man were represented in various places even though they didn't understand what they were drawing. It was fascinating to see all the mysteries and secrets right in front of us.

The *Malkhut* is not attached to the other spiritual points in the body, only to the *Yesod*. This is because everything culminates in the *Yesod* and from there passes into the *Malkhut* and then into the face of the earth so it can bring a change to creation. The planetary systems, including the sun, moon and stars, are also connected into the body. I have grandbabies who used to battle with sleep during a full moon. Children with various issues and challenges will play up during a full moon and patients in a psychiatric ward will be more difficult to deal with during that time period as well. God made the planetary system so they're not demonic; we've got to learn how to live above the sun in order to govern these systems that sit and resonate within us.

Psalm 19 says, "To the chief musician, a Psalm of David. The heavens declare the glory of God and the firmament or stars show His handiwork. Day unto day they utter speech and night unto night they reveal knowledge." The stars utter knowledge and tell us secrets. I used to look at the stars and tell them that any time they wanted to speak to me, I was ready to listen. Nothing happened until I realised that the structure of their frequency was within me and that I could engage with them in that realm. When there was an attempted Coup in South Africa,

Mars and Saturn were in alignment. Mars, in its unredeemed form, is the warring planet and crazy things were happening in various parts of the country.

Somebody then said that they felt we needed to look at the star system. Mars was positioned in a particular place, and Jupiter, which was to bring peace, was in another place and above them was the Lion of Judah. Yahweh told us that if we engaged with Him, He would overshadow the planetary system of war and bring peace to the nation. That planetary system was only in alignment for three days, so while we were engaging and praying in the Spirit on that Monday, I announced that it would all be over within three days. On the fourth day, as we engaged with that system, bringing it above the sun, these Beings or Watchers came out of the East gate and said, "We will remove the confusion which is over the minds of the people," and on that day it was all over and the looting ended.

On one occasion I was taken up to a star. It had a big black hole in it and as I stood there, I didn't know what I was supposed to do with it. I put my hand out and felt the rim of the star and then I put my head into the hole. It was so dark in that hole that I thought it was going to swallow me. I called out 'hello?' and my echo went on and on into this cavernous place. When I told Ian about my encounter with this 'hollow' star, he said that I was supposed to redeem it. We are able to go back to the encounters we have had so I went back to that star which was still in the same place waiting for me. As a spirit-man I opened up and let the light/*yechida* come out of me and as I did that, the light ate up the darkness. I heard a 'ping' sound and the star started to sing. It had its sound back. We all have a star and when we find our way to it that pathway remains open and we can go there by intent, desire and faith.

When a group of us were on the ship in Norway to engage with the North Gate, Ian was not well at all. Two days later he was preaching in his session and said he was fine. When I asked him how he felt better so quickly he said that he went into his DNA, looked into his autosomes, found what was causing the problem and pulled it out. He prayed in the Spirit while he was working through his DNA and within two days, he was healed. I had a health issue so decided to change my diet. I started taking different supplements as well as doing cold water therapy because I knew this would realign my autoimmune system. While I was dunking myself in really freezing water, I would see my hand go through my DNA, and by faith, I would find the offending thing, grab hold of it, pull it out of my DNA and wash it down the drain. I kept doing that until I was completely healed.

We cannot deal into other people's DNA, they have to do it themselves, but I do believe that at some stage in the future we will understand the technology required to be able to bring healing to people through their DNA. At the moment we are able to pray for the sick and lay hands on them and they will recover.

Chapter 3
The Cube - Part One

We're not obliged to engage with the *Sefirot*, but I do believe that knowledge is power, however our access into the Kingdom realms and to Yahweh is always through the blood of Yeshua. I do like the fact that I know where everything is inside of me, I know what it does and I know where to find it in Scripture. I don't subscribe to the shallow Christian explanations anymore because I much prefer to know how things are connected into the Tree of Life. I've seen Jewish people engaging with various formats in order to enter in and walk the *Sefirot*. We do not have to do that because we can go in through the blood of the Lamb. However, we do honour the mysteries that they have kept for us because these mysteries have become our foundation from which we can reach into the secrets of Yahweh.

Since I started exploring the cube some time ago, I've come to love it. Many of us have seen drawings of a cube with a lot of other things depicted inside it which can look confusing but a friend explained it very well – He said, "The cube is simple. You sit inside it and operate it from within." That's when I understood the concept. In the *Sepher Yetzirah* it is called the Cube of Space.

The cube is called the Cube of Space. Sacred Geometry is fundamental in nature and has five platonic solids hidden inside of it symbolising the underlying geometric patterns found throughout our universe. All of them correlate to the cube because it simply facilitates the flow of energy in creation. It's the basic building block of humanity as well as the universe and makes up the elements of fire, air, water, earth and ether. The cube, which is six-sided, has four doors, one on each corner. It has an upside and a downside, or North and South, and it has an East and a West. The Jews draw the twenty-two Hebrew letters on the corners of the cube and also on the middle lines because of the energy which flows between every letter. Sacred Geometry, which is a mystical form of geometry, ascribed symbolic and sacred meanings to certain geometric shapes and proportions. They say that God is the geometer of the world and if the whole of creation, according to scientists, is created using shapes and geometry, then we should also be looking at it in a spiritual way.

The *Sefer Yetzirah* or Book of Creation is one that I use regularly and it describes how the Jews interpret and operate with the *Mazzaroth*, or the Zodiac. I don't like using the word 'Zodiac' because it is apparently 12.5 degrees off where it should be, in its corrupted state, after the fall of Lucifer.

I now see the *Mazzaroth* as a wheel within a wheel whereas before, it was just a circle with symbols placed around it. To a Jew everything is circular and everything comes back to itself. When we read the book of Revelation, it speaks about Zion being built like a cube upon a cube.

Many years ago, a beautiful book was written about a missionary in Asia who had an orphanage. The orphans were having out of body experiences and going to Heaven while lying on the floor and speaking in another language. When they came back from Heaven, they would talk about the Seven Spirits and about the many rooms within the dimensions of God. These were illiterate children who didn't know a thing about Heaven. They also described the cubes that they saw while they were there. These children couldn't read the Bible, so they didn't know that Heaven looked like that.

I wanted to understand the function of the cube better, so I drew it as if I were sitting inside the core and matrix of the cube. My natural and carnal bodies are here on earth. My carnal body is the flesh and blood body that everyone can see while my natural body, which looks like me, is also seen on the face of the earth. A friend of mine told me about the time her mom was in hospital dying of cancer. Her mom kept asking her why I was in the bed next to her. At the time, I was praying for her but I wasn't in the room with her even though she kept insisting that I was. What she saw was my natural body; it looks like me and it travels here and there on the earth busy with assignments. When Peter came out of jail and knocked on the door the people there said it was just Peter's angel which means that they were used to this sort of thing happening.

St. Francis Xavier was on a ship that ran into trouble. A number of those on the ship boarded a rowing boat and were set adrift. After a while the ship was out of sight and they were frantic as they were now lost at sea. St. Xavier gave them courage and told them to not despair because they would be saved. Three days later everyone rejoiced as they spotted the ship on the horizon. As the people were being taken on board they were looking for the Preacher who had been with them in the rowing boat. The sailors said that Francis Xavier had been on the ship the entire three days and told them not to despair because they would find the rowing boat. Francis Xavier was once seen in six different places at the same time, in his physical form. It was his natural body, not his carnal form.

You also have a spiritual body which is the one that is seated with Christ in heavenly places. Here you are seated on your mountain of government and where you put on Christ. This is the place where you, as spirit, with a soul and body come into divine sovereignty with the Father, Son and Holy Spirit.

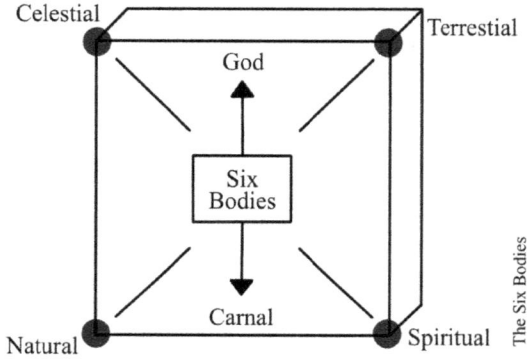

Your terrestrial body travels to and fro on the face of the earth and does not look like you but it does carry the essence of who you are. If I saw you in your terrestrial body, I would recognise you instantly even though it might not necessarily look like your carnal body. The terrestrial body is the one which sees what is going to happen, for instance a volcano erupting or an earthquake happening.

Your celestial body is the one which is busy going about the Father's business in the celestial arena with the sun, moon and stars, because we are here for signs, seasons, days and years.

When our five bodies — carnal, natural, spiritual, terrestrial and celestial — come into divine union with one another, we have a sixth body which manifests as a God-body. The New Covenant is written in the blood of the Lamb and this blood gives us the boldness to enter in through the veil. The cube is both on the inside of us and on the outside so we can begin to arc with our spiritual body, through the blood of the Lamb. I don't like using the word 'ascend' because it makes it sound as if I'm always trying to reach up into something that's just out of my grasp. When I arc with my bodies, I'm creating the God-body within me so that it manifests from within who I am while I'm governing from my seat of rest within the cube.

Quantum physics is fascinating. You can take one photon and place it on one side of the earth and then take another photon and place it on the opposite side of the earth and when you move one of them, the other one will also move. In the past I would feel that something was not right and I would say that Holy Spirit was prompting me to intercede. Now I understand, that because of this divine connection between all my bodies, my terrestrial body sees something that is happening on the face of the earth and it warns my carnal and natural bodies which then feel it too.

An important factor when dealing with the cube is to understand how the six bodies operate within it. When I'm asleep and dreaming, I, as a spirit, can feel my soul go into the realms of the Kingdom. When we come back, we stand next to my body whilst it's sleeping and tell my body to wake up because there is legislation to be done.

The four corners of the cube are four doors which correlate to the Hebrew letter *Dalet* because its gematria is four. We enter the door of the cube within us to arc with our spiritual and celestial bodies so we can see what they are doing in the different dimensions — these dimensions sit within us. If we learn to be aware of our other bodies, then we've understood this dimension.

When my terrestrial body sees something, my carnal body senses it because I'm quantumly entangled although I might not readily recognise what it means. A while ago, I saw the Hawaiians putting their hands up and asking for help. Their flag was flying upside down which meant their country was in distress. When my terrestrial body saw this, my carnal and natural bodies also started to feel that something was going to happen. We began to engage and two days later there was a devastating earthquake on the island. I enquired of Yahweh why this had happened despite us engaging. Even though the volcano erupted we were able to go into the Kingdom realms and legislate some things and set a boundary.

Before I learned all this new terminology, I would have said something like, "The Holy Spirit gave me a prompting in my spirit that something was going to happen in Hawaii." Now, I believe that my terrestrial body saw it, and because of quantum entanglement, warned my natural and carnal bodies. While I was still pastoring, I was in a church meeting in Johannesburg which is about 600km from Durban, my home town. I wanted to check in with my church so I just closed my eyes and started to engage and it literally felt as though I was standing at the back of my church. I saw all the people busy with their various activities in the meeting. I then heard the pastor of the Johannesburg church calling my name and I felt myself come back into my body. It was an amazing experience! On my way home I received a call from my daughter saying that she didn't know what I had been up to that morning, but two people had just approached her asking to speak to me because they had both seen me at the back of the hall.

I told her to ask them what they had seen me wearing and they both described my outfit. They had seen my natural body. On another occasion I was in South Africa and wanted to make sure that the folk in the UK were doing well while I was away. I saw myself amongst the trees looking in through the window when a young boy in the group saw me. Almost immediately I received a text message from his mother saying that he had just seen me. I asked what he had seen me wearing and he correctly told her. I've purposely engaged with all of my bodies on numerous occasions.

Ian Clayton's wife, was instrumental in encouraging him to formulate protocols on how to engage with various Beings and also to frame terminology for what we've encountered so that we can have understanding. Sometimes, a person will insist that they have met you but you don't actually know them. It could either be that they've met one of your other bodies or that they knew you when you were both illuminaries in the heart of Yahweh. When Jesus was on the Mount of Transfiguration I believe all six of His bodies came together and manifested His God-body. That is our goal, to manifest all our bodies so that we manifest the God-body on the outside and the physical body on the inside.

When we read *Matthew 17:2* in Hebrew, it says that the disciples looked at His face and it became 'other.' In Greek, 'transfigured' is metamorphoo which means to change into another form. They could see it was Him but His face looked like something else because He'd taken on His God-body. After His resurrection, on the road to Emmaus, the travellers didn't know who He was. When He was in His God-body in the garden, Mary didn't know who He was until He spoke, and because she knew His voice, she recognized Him.

I believe that Enoch knew how to bring all of his bodies together and operate in the God-body so he could travel up and down. I believe Elijah did it too because he was able to go up and down and in and out. When the whirlwind took Elijah up in a chariot, the prophets asked Elisha if they could go and look for him but he said no. They went anyway and spent three days looking for him. Why would they have spent three days looking for him unless they knew that Elijah was able to 'jump' or to translocate?

Once, Ian was standing at the edge of the known universe and he called out, "I want to know you." A Being appeared and followed him back into this realm. At the time, Ian didn't know who or what it was and thought it was perhaps a trans-dimensional Being. I actually saw that Being around Ian myself and when I told Ian, he said that I should have introduced myself. The second time I saw the same 30-foot-high Being, he looked at me, so I introduced myself. He just nodded his head.

Two years ago, as we began to understand who and what we were and where we came from, Ian said to me, "Do you know who that Being was?" I replied that I did; it was Ian, in his original illuminary form, who had been with Yahweh before he came onto the face of the earth. I've met my original form once and although it doesn't sound like me, it is me. I remember thinking how odd it was that I'm so small here on earth while the other me is 30-foot high. I'm not sure yet what we're supposed to do with our illuminary body, which is our original blueprint.

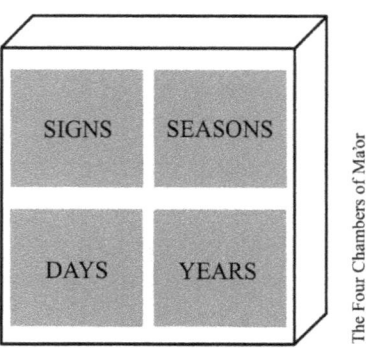

In *Genesis 1:14-15* we read, "And God said, 'let there be lights in the firmament of the heaven to divide the day from the night; and let them be for signs, and for seasons, and for days, and years: and let them be for lights in the firmament of the heaven to give light upon the earth': and it was so." The Hebrew word for 'lights' is *ma'or* meaning luminary/lumination.

The separation of the day and night does not mean the difference between sunshine and night time. It's about taking the day, where we walk out the secrets, and dividing it from the night, where we found the mysteries. So, night and day or light and dark is about secrets and mysteries being revealed into light. *Genesis 1:16* says, "And God made two great lights; the greater light to rule the day, and the lesser light to rule the night: He made the stars also." The greater light is a sun which rules the day and the working out of the mysteries, while the lesser light is the moon which we see shining in the sky. Illuminaries were in the firmament before the sun and the stars were created and our illuminary body is the one that will change the face of the earth because it's the one that creation is groaning for.

There are so many never-ending mysteries and secrets in Yahweh because He is an ever-moving horizon. In fact, the Zohar says that the upper portions of who God is feed into the lower waters and teach the lower waters, within God, who He is, which lead the Rabbis to understand that God is an ever moving horizon with no end – He is constantly expanding. When the 200 sons of God/Watchers saw the daughters of men on the earth, they took wives for themselves and had offspring who were called the Men of Renown. The fallen angels have no hope of salvation or of redemption because they were not made with human DNA. We were made in His image and out of the dust of the earth. When they fell He said to them, "You have fallen, and you thought you saw the secrets and the mysteries, but the ones you saw were worthless and you've given them to the women. Because of you, men and women create havoc on the face of the earth."

Just like not all of the human race is evil, so too, not all of the Nephilim seed is evil. Some of them are the good Watchers. The good ones are 30-foot giants while the smaller ones are of mixed seed. David met a group of men who were Men of Renown or *gibborim* and were between 12 and 15 foot-tall like Goliath had been. In *2 Samuel 23:8-38* David hired them to be part of his personal army and even made them rulers over Israel. He would not have let 'mixed-seed' people rule over Israel unless he knew how to change their DNA and redeem them. Their DNA could be changed because they had human and angelic DNA in them however, I don't believe that we should be going into the underworld and winning other Beings to Jesus. Let's concentrate on what's on the earth and leave the rest to God.

There's a good chance we all have a touch of mixed-seed in us. I wasn't delighted to discover that I had alien seed in my family lineage and in my DNA. These mixed-seed races are still among us today but have reduced in size to blend in. They can be redeemed because human DNA is involved.

I know people who have walked in phenomenal power but because they carried the pain of being fatherless, they dabbled in things they should not have touched and engaged with gates that they should have never opened. The North, West and South gates are not ready to be opened or redeemed so we must not touch them until it is their time and season.

When we open certain realms, we can walk into apostasy where we then trample underfoot the blood of Jesus which we read in *Hebrews 10:29* and it's very hard to come back from that place.

I'm becoming very aware of the fact that my bodies can travel, so when I'm sensing something, I ask myself which body is seeing the thing that I'm sensing and then I start to arc with that particular body. I'm concentrating on seeing my future and pulling my present, and who I am in the physical, into the future, so that I can operate from the future into the present.

Recently, my plane was delayed by half an hour and I only had fifteen minutes to get off one plane and on to another plane all the while dealing with COVID protocols, masks, permission letters for travelling, customs and passport control! I disembarked at gate D33 and I had to embark at gate D71. I started to panic a bit and then suddenly knew what to do – I stood where I was and spoke to Time. I put my rod (like the rod of Moses) into the ground and said, "Listen to me, Time. I don't serve you, you serve me." I began to pull Time towards me and said I would not stress because all the people waiting in front of me were not going to take longer than ten minutes. I also didn't look at my watch. I was taking all of my bodies and pulling them into my future and telling Time that it had 10 minutes to get me to the front of the queue. When I looked at my watch ten minutes later, I was standing in front of the ground hostess who didn't even ask for any of my paperwork and I got to the boarding gate with ten minutes to spare!

I'm very conscious of the frequency that words carry so I never say things like, "Oh my gosh, I can't believe it's Christmas already! I can't believe how this year has flown by!" Time doesn't fly and I refuse to allow it to go too fast because I haven't given it permission to go fast. Each number on the clock face, from one to twelve, has an angel that governs over that particular time. One day, I had many things that I needed to get done so I told Time to stop making my day run away with me. I governed Time and managed to fit everything in before the end of business that day. If we don't do this, we will be governed by Time which places us under the sun. Time also causes us to age until we eventually die if we don't govern properly. It's only above the sun that this ageing process stops because we live from a different place.

I cut the soul ties I had with the sun and the moon and I told them that they could not govern over me any longer. When I did that, I saw myself really huge and the moon was so tiny in comparison. It has no effect on me anymore. Living above the sun means that we live above the seed-line of decay which lies in man's morality and we begin to look at what Yahweh has for us. We can take the cube and the Tree of Life above the sun and sit within our God-man status while we also arc with ourselves on the face of the earth. We do this because everything you and I do is about changing creation. Yahweh loves the earth and it is the diadem in the middle of His crown. The three different creations are mentioned in *Genesis chapters 1-5* and Scripture shows us that Yahweh didn't destroy the earth but kept replenishing it by putting man back onto it. He loves the earth so much that we are going to make a new heaven and a new earth.

Proverbs 8 mentions dimensions that existed even before the beginning of time as we know it. They are:

- Eternal realm
- Beginning of His ways
- His works of old
- Everlasting
- Beginning
- Creation

These are over and above the seven heavens which are:

- Kingdom of Earth
- Kingdom of God
- Kingdom of Heaven
- Heaven
- Heaven of Heavens
- Perfection
- Eternity

Each one of these Heavens have seven other realms which totals forty-nine Heavens.

There are many other created Beings that live in these realms. In *Proverbs 8:22-31* we read, "The Lord possessed me at the beginning of His way, before His works of old. I have been established from everlasting, from the beginning, before there was ever an earth. When there were no depths I was brought forth, when there were no fountains abounding with water. Before the mountains were settled, before the hills, I was brought forth; while as yet He had not made the earth or the fields, or the primal dust of the world. When He prepared the heavens, I was there, when He drew a circle on the face of the deep, when He established the clouds above, when He strengthened the fountains of the deep, when He assigned to the sea its limit, so that the waters would not transgress His command, when He marked out the foundations of the earth, then I was beside Him as a master craftsman; and I was daily His delight, rejoicing always before Him, rejoicing in His inhabited world, and my delight was with the sons of men."

The Beings and Everliving Ones existed before the beginning. As Illuminaries who were with Yahweh, He placed us in the heavens where we divided the day from the night and were there for signs and seasons, days and years. During the Beginning we have the 7 days as mentioned in Genesis.

Within the 8th day, Lucifer, hasatan and the great dragon fell. Then came the flood and after that, during the days of Peleg, the earths separated and moved dimensionally. There are planets hundreds of thousands of light years away that look very similar to our earth. There are some planets in other dimensions which are home to different Beings, for example Atlantis and there is a place where the *tachashim* or unicorns, which are large, ritually pure animals with one horn live.

The earth is currently in its fourth estate. While living on the earth we are able to arc with our other bodies so that we can operate in the other realms. We agreed to pass through the Mazzaroth, and then through all the other realms, to come into our mother's womb. Our voice creates a pathway so that we can find our way back, to before the beginning, when we were with Yahweh. When we meditate on the *Yod Hey Vav Hey* we are reaching through all of these realms, into the secrets of Yahweh, to release them back into creation.

As mentioned before, Adam was clothed with flesh (or skins) by Yahweh. I believe he was a light-being. The Book of Jasher says that when he died, his skins were passed down generationally until Nimrod came in possession of them. When he put them on he became a powerful man who hunted the Nephilim, a mixed-seed race of giants, who were causing havoc on the face of the earth. Initially, Nimrod shut the portals but part of his generation decided that they wanted to build a tower where they could practice sacred geometry. They called this tower 'Babble' or 'Babel.' The Book of Jasher records that when they opened this portal, which would take them back to Eden, they saw angels watching them and started shooting arrows up at them. The angels caught the arrows and threw them back down.

At that point, God just changed their frequency and they could no longer operate because they were no longer in unity. We've been taught that they were building a high structure to get to God but this is not possible. Instead, they were in the process of building a portal, through sacred geometry. This is still evident in the pyramids today which were apparently covered in gold and were all built on the same ley lines. When the mixed-seed lineage came into being things began to be corrupted.

Ley lines are spiritual lines on which we can traverse around the face of the earth but they've been hijacked by the demonic. When I see a ley line, I just cover it with the blood of the Lamb and then no devil or witch on the face of the earth can use it after that.

The New Testament says that we are fitly joined together and set on a Chief Cornerstone. Why is Yeshua called a Chief Cornerstone? It's because all of us, as cubes, are being built into a building and coming together in unity, with Him as our chief cornerstone. We're a house of living stones, not rocks or blobs and we're moving like wheels within wheels with everyone in his place, without chaos, which we read in *1 Peter 2:6*. If we all came into unity, what would we be capable of?

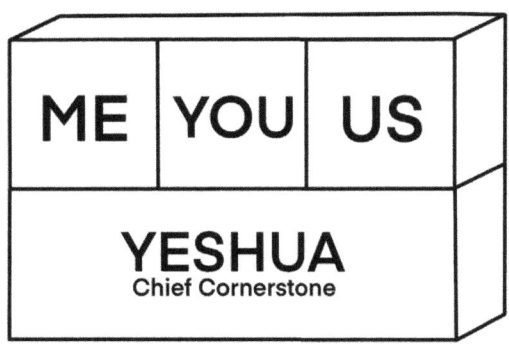

There are many unknown mysteries, millions of years old, that are connected to sacred geometry and we now know that it exists within us in the form of a cube. The earth also operates within the context of the cube and the seven different Kingdoms of Heaven are part of it as well.

Paul mentions the cube in *Ephesians 3:18-20*: "… May be able to comprehend with all the saints what is the width and length and depth and height— to know the love of Christ which passes knowledge; that you may be filled with all the fullness of God."

Why would Paul talk about my maturity and my call in Yeshua in an upwards; downwards; backwards and forwards manner? As a Pharisee, he was teaching from a place of understanding the cube. The cube of maturity looks like this: It's the unfolding of our mountain so that we know who and what we are.

When we reach into the seat of rest from the mountain of the government of Yahweh within, which is the God-man, we can see the height of our calling, the depth of our calling and the breadth of our calling in Christ Jesus. We look at the past and then push it into the future where we take hold of that and bring it into our present.

When we extend our tent pegs, as found in *Isaiah 54:2*, we're extending them from the four corners of the cube of maturity. We're reaching into the *Olam*, which is the future, and we bring it into our present by taking our tent pegs and expanding our mountain of government within us to reach into more capacity. This cube of maturity will take us into the place of sonship and into priesthood in the 13th Age. Jesus was the 12th priesthood and we are the 13th and final priesthood and we will build a New Heaven and a New Earth.

The same principle applies when I look at Love. There is Justice and Judgement on one side; Grace and Mercy on the other. These four pillars make up Love and the minute I saw that I knew that this was a cube because there is always a formula. The four pillars of Love are four Beings which I am able to engage with within the cube of who I am. I am then able to put this Love within a cube on the inside of myself and I start to reach up and down into the height and the depth of the love that Yeshua has for me. The Rabbis know that within the Tree of Life there is Justice and Judgement, Grace and Mercy.

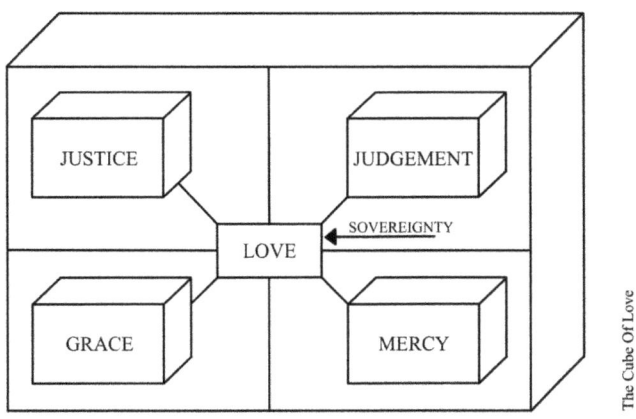

I can place the cube and the Tree of Life into almost anything that is within me and then learn how to govern it from within myself. *Revelation 21:16* says, "And the city lieth foursquare, and the length is as large as the breadth." That means heaven is built in the shape of a square or cube. The holy of holies, which is the inner sanctuary of the tabernacle where Shekinah appeared, is built in the shape of a cube as seen in *Ezekiel 41:4*.

How can we govern over our bodies for the restoration of health? I believe that Yahweh is teaching us how to heal ourselves. Praying in the Spirit is one of the ways to bring healing; another way is to understand the role of the blood of Yeshua in communion. Cold water therapy shocks your autoimmune system back into shape while natural supplements and oils also help. Ian Clayton has been teaching about going into our DNA and autosomes. All of these modalities are working towards the restoration of our bodies.

Chapter 4
The Cube - Part Two

In creation, nothing is placed in a haphazard fashion because everything works according to lines, patterns and functions within the cube which facilitates the flow of energy through the platonic solids of fire, air, water, earth and ether. Scripture records that we are stones, fitly joined together and properly set upon each other — it's not done in a chaotic manner.

The Hebrew people have kept the mysteries of Yahweh for a long time which have now become our stepping stone into the secrets of Yahweh. The whole issue of night and day was not to separate the light from the dark; it was so that we could enter into the dark cloud of the Lord in order to access the mysteries and to reveal them in the light. We sleep at night in order to access the mysteries and reveal them into the day, through the Womb of the Morning, as morning stars.

Scripture makes reference to the waters in *Genesis 1*. Water is everywhere; we even have upper and lower waters within our bodies. The Living Letter, *Mem*, positions itself between our two hip bones and our belly button area is where the upper and lower waters are separated; it's up to us to bring them into balance. The upper waters are found above the sun in the Kingdom realms. The lower waters are below the sun. They have been kept for us so that we can access the secrets situated in the upper waters. I don't believe that the secrets are accessible outside of the blood of the Lamb as we have to pass through the veil of His flesh. I believe that the decade of the 2020's is the timeframe available to us to learn how to deal with our junk and how to deal with our bodies. It is also a time for us to reach into the upper waters, as illuminaries, to access the secrets of Yahweh which enable us to do what we do.

The 2030's are going to be interesting; there has been talk of the magnetic North shifting. When Lucifer fell, the North and South magnetic poles shifted and depending on which translation we read, Isaiah records that the earth shook, wobbled, jumped and moved. There is talk that the poles are going to shift back which will result in some chaos happening on the face of the earth. For this reason, I believe that as we mature in Yahweh during this next decade, we will be able to deal into that very easily and by the 2030's we will know how to access the realms of His Kingdom to be able to gather without having to use the media which is currently available in the Babylonian system. I believe we're going to be able to meet in the classrooms of Heaven.

In *Matthew 28:16-19* we read, "Then the eleven disciples went away into Galilee, to the mountain which Jesus had appointed for them. When they saw Him, they worshiped Him; but some doubted." I've been to Galilee; there are rolling hills there but definitely no mountains. The original text says that they went **into** the mountain, not **onto** the mountain, to wait for Him. This speaks about going into a place of government. When the disciples saw Him coming, the Bible says that some doubted. I've often wondered if this doubting had something to do with them wondering where they were. Then He spoke to them and told them to make disciples of all the nations, baptising in the name of the Father, Son and Holy Spirit. Christians call this the Great Commission. When I looked that passage up in the original language, that Great Commission is not about water baptism, rather it's about what we're doing today, being baptized into the full knowledge of the Father, Yeshua and the *Ruach* *haKodesh*.

We are busy doing the Great Commission.

When the word 'mountain' is mentioned in Scripture, it refers to a place of government. In *Psalm 24:3* we read, "Who shall ascend into the hill of the Lord or the mountain of the Lord? He who has clean hands and a pure heart." This is an access point into a place of government; it's not just sitting on a hill, waiting for Jesus to come along. The Great Commission was to baptise people into the full knowledge of the secrets of the Father and the Son and the Holy Spirit and does not pertain to water baptism.

There are other Scriptures which specifically address water baptism. The Jews do seventeen different baptisms while we do eight of them. Yochanan, or John the Baptist as we refer to him, was not a baptiser; he was the legitimate High Priest who performed the baptism of repentance, called a *mikvah*, which is why the people went out to see him.

We must know how to heal ourselves and how to walk in divine health before we can actually learn how to heal others and I believe that divine health is another key that Yahweh is going to show us how to use. We will then operate in the things that we've always dreamed of doing, like walking past a cripple person and telling them to rise to their feet and walk.

We must also understand the five-part nature of man, because when we understand all of our bodies, and how they culminate in the 6th body, the God-body, we will put on what looks like the Enochian body where we will be able to go up and down, in and out, accessing the realms of the Kingdom.

There are various Scriptures that mention our different bodies and Paul said in *1 Corinthians 5:3*, "For I verily, though absent in body but present in spirit, have judged already as though I were present concerning him who hath so done this deed." He meant it when he said that his spiritual (or even his natural body) was there. He was in jail at the time but he was also in Corinth. Instead of saying, "I feel in my spirit that such and such is happening," or, "The Holy Spirit showed me that this would happen," or, "I sense something," we should be turning to our bodies and finding out which one is the one talking to us and then arc with it.

1 Corinthians 15:39-45 says the following, "All flesh is not the same flesh, but there is one kind of flesh of men, another flesh of animals, another of fish, and another of birds. There are also celestial bodies and terrestrial bodies; but the glory of the celestial is one, and the glory of the terrestrial is another. There is one glory of the sun, another glory of the moon, and another glory of the stars; for one star differs from another star in glory. So also is the resurrection of the dead. The body is sown in corruption, it is raised in incorruption. It is sown in dishonour, it is raised in glory. It is sown in weakness, it is raised in power. It is sown a natural body, it is raised a spiritual body. There is a natural body, and there is a spiritual body. And so it is written, 'The first man Adam became a living being.' The last Adam became a life-giving spirit."

Before I met Ian Clayton I had no one I could talk to about the crazy things I saw and did. When I met Ian I told him that I saw my husband the day after he transitioned and he said that was quite normal. I didn't expect that reply so I began to tell him some of the other things that I did. When I'm on a long flight (I get bored easily) I sit in a place of contemplation and then I 'step out' of the plane and ride out into the clouds on my 'surfboard'. He told me not to call it a surfboard but to call it a dais! It's encrusted with diamonds and precious stones and is a transportation tool. I was so excited that he knew what I was talking about! We all know the story of Aladdin and how he travels on a flying carpet. The mysteries are in plain sight!

I wrote a children's book called The Other Christmas Story and in it I mention the Wise Men who were God-men that came out of the East gate, not out from the East or from Persia. Twelve God-men came through but only nine came into the face of the earth while the other three stayed behind. The other three are now traversing the face of the earth, but they didn't do so at the beginning. Nine of them came through and followed the star by using sacred geometry in order to find the Messiah. Google will tell you that camels were not ridden in Israel at the time of Yeshua's birth. They were beasts of burden, yes, but they were not used for human transportation so the picture we have of three men riding camels and bringing three little presents for a king is just bizarre. Most of our Christmas doctrine comes from Christmas cards and not from the Bible.

We say that Jesus was born in a stable and yet, in all four gospels, the stable isn't even mentioned. It just so happens that He was put in a manger, which was probably hewn out of rock, inside a cave. The God-men would have been travelling on what looked like flying carpets, which were their daises, and this caught the king's attention. Back in those days, they were able to do crazy things through astrology and astronomy so they were used to doing and seeing unusual things. We see this when Moses went back to Pharaoh's court; the wizards or sorcerers threw their rods down which turned into snakes. Moses was not perturbed as he had grown up in that environment and was used to it.

Having a God-body is a secret that we need to understand. In fact, the book of Jasher says that Enoch would go in and out of a portal which they called The Ends of the Earth. There came a time when the elders asked him to stop coming through the portal because they were terrified of His countenance — he had fully taken on his God-body. It was the same thing with Moses when the people told him to cover his face. One of the manuscripts I read says that the people died when they looked at Moses showing the four faces of Yahweh. He would raise them from the dead and when they looked at him again they would die again. That's when they asked him to cover his face.

The book of Enoch has been translated and compiled into four books from various scroll fragments that include parts of the book of Noah which records the events of his birth. He was born with white hair, his eyes shone so that they lit up the room and he was able to speak and glorify God. At this point, Lamech his father, went to find his own father, Methuselah, and told him what had happened, saying that he didn't think the child was his but that he had been sent from the realm of heaven. Methuselah told Lamech to go and speak to his own father, Enoch. Lamech went to the Ends of the Earth, which is a portal, called for Enoch and told him that his wife had given birth to a son that was completely different to everyone else. At that time, there was no one who was not of mixed seed except for Noah which we read about in *Genesis 6:9*. Enoch replied that Noah had been with him and that he had been sent, as an insertion, because a deluge was coming and he was going to save mankind.

Throughout Scripture, we see other insertions — Enoch; Rahab; David; Mary, the mother of Yeshua and Yeshua Himself among many. In other words, the Father had to insert pure seed by the Holy Spirit. There is belief that these insertions didn't stop at the birth of Yeshua and that there will be more. Mary, the mother of Yeshua, is a very interesting person. Her parents were childless but even so, they would go to the temple as was their custom to pray to conceive. Eventually, they fell pregnant with Mary and soon after she was weaned, they dedicated her to work and serve in the temple.

A friend of mine was given permission to take a photo of a painting in Israel which shows the High Priests offering sacrifices in the Holy Place. Standing behind them is a little girl of about five years of age and this, I believe, is the mother of Yeshua. When I had an encounter with Mary, she told me that she always knew that her purpose in life was to carry the Messiah. She was of pure seed and belonged to the royal household along with Joseph, whom she married. Rahab was called 'the harlot' because when the King James version was written they didn't know how else to describe her when they had to translate that she was 'in the house of men'. The Bible says that she took the two spies and hid them in a basket in her house, when in fact, the original writings say that she hid them in *isha*, which in Hebrew is the word for woman. She hid them within herself in another dimension and when the soldiers had gone she let them out again.

A similar thing happened with Noah while he was in the Ark/box/cube. In *Genesis 8:13,* we read how Noah removed the covering. What covering was that? People have said it was a tarpaulin, or a piece of wood but there's no Scripture that describes what it was other than saying it was *miksê* which was the same coverings of the skins of the tabernacle. When the Ark settled on the mountain, Noah lifted the dove out of himself so that it could go and find dry land. The dove couldn't find any dry land and it returned to the Ark where Noah took it back **into** himself, not onto his shoulder. Noah had become the covering through which the dove could leave and enter. Where was the Ark situated while they couldn't find dry land for more than a year? It must have been in the upper waters. Where were the Jews when they were in the wilderness for 40 years and couldn't find their way out? They were not on the face of the earth; they were in the upper waters.

I had been practicing how to arc with all my bodies when my son contacted me (I was living in another country) and told me that he was fine so I could stop checking in on him. I went, with my natural body, to my granddaughter while she was asleep and spoke to her. The next day I phoned her to ask if she saw me during the night. She normally said no, but that she did see grandpa Ron. I keep on practicing because I want her to become as aware of me as she is of him. Her little brother, who was 14 months old, kept picking up pictures of his grandpa Ron and bringing them to us. Their parents keep his photographs in the house so that when he visits them, they know who he is.

This activation also works with animals and the Jews teach that all animals spoke. The king of the beasts was not a lion; it was a standing, walking, talking, snake, and when it spoke to Eve she didn't run away in fright because she was used to the animals communicating with her. In today's world, we have animal whisperers who have accessed the ability to communicate with animals. It can still be done.

I am learning how to look into the future and engage with it. During one of the COVID 'waves', I was travelling between various countries and sincerely hoped I wouldn't get stuck in another lockdown where I would have to isolate for many days. I engaged with my future to see if I could see myself in Ireland and when I did, I phoned my travel agent and asked her to book my tickets. I did the same thing when I intended travelling to Norway. It is one of the most expensive countries in the world, so I didn't want my family to book an Airbnb if I wasn't able to travel because of restrictions. I started to engage until I could smell Norway. I could smell the wood, I could smell the coffee, so I called my son and asked him to book the Airbnb because I saw myself going to visit them.

This could be called déjà vu as it aptly describes us, living from our future. Time, as we know it, does not exist in those realms so it's possible to arc into the future without realizing it and one day we go somewhere and really feel like we've been there before. We actually have been there before because our other bodies have already engaged in that place and we're having a déjà vu moment.

My mom used to have out-of-body experiences all the time where she would watch her body while it was attached to a silver cord. She never tried to do this deliberately and it used to disturb her greatly. One of my great-great-uncles was a white witch and many of my relatives did strange things.
When I became born again from above, I prayed and broke that thing off her and she stopped having those out-of-body experiences. Everybody can access their silver cord which allows us to move to and fro on the face of the earth but it does not allow us to go up and down. When we get born again however, that silver cord gets cut and we receive the golden bowl which sits in the centre of the menorah on the inside of us. That bowl has oil in it which never runs dry and is the *yechida* which is what we use to traverse up and down and to and fro. Only those who are born again by the Blood can gain access to this realm. *Ecclesiastes 12:6-7* says, "Remember your Creator before the silver cord is loosed, or the golden bowl is broken, or the pitcher shattered at the fountain, or the wheel broken at the well. Then the dust will return to the earth as it was, and the spirit will return to God who gave it."

I've done ministry with people who have experienced trauma. Sometimes I take them down their timeline in their DNA, all the way back into the womb, to see what happened at specific times so that healing can take place. When they revisit that time and place in their DNA, they always see Jesus standing in the middle of the trauma with them. I once ministered to a girl who was raped and she struggled to go back to that time and place. She absolutely had to do it, for her own sake, so eventually she conceded. It was very traumatic for her. While she was in that place I asked her to look around and tell me what she saw. She saw Jesus standing right by her head telling her that He would not leave her and that she would be okay. Because of that, she received complete emotional healing once she realized she had not been alone at all. Her biggest trauma was the fact that she had felt abandoned.

I believe that Yahweh shows us things from our past within our DNA strand so that we can bring it into our present to receive healing by the blood of the Lamb so that we can step into our future. That door is always open so we can go back into our DNA and fix it.

When we have repetitive dreams or encounters, it's generally because we haven't interpreted the situation correctly and we need to find the real reason behind it. When this happens, we're not only engaging with our DNA but also with cellular memory which can go as far back as 4000 BC and beyond. Yahweh wants to take us back to that point to redeem something. I've gone right back in time to the 13th and 18th Centuries, to deal into things that happened on the trading floors of those timelines that had embedded themselves in my cellular memory. The rest have just been DNA issues that I've had to deal into. I've seen my DNA rise with a trading floor jutting out of its side and was able to deal into issues which included free masonry, the Jezebel spirit and Druidry, which were all things that Yahweh showed me.

If anything in my DNA accuses my family line or myself, then I take it to the Mobile Court. When I opened the door of the trading floor in my DNA in the 13th Century, I saw the trading floor that had a menhir lying on its side. My ancestors were there and they were trading with some druids. As I opened that door, they all turned and looked at me and I heard Yahweh tell me that I HAD to get papers in order to deal with what I saw. I quickly shut the door, went to the Mobile Court and told Yahweh that there was an accusation against my family line. I asked Him to forgive me on behalf of my family, I received my papers and dashed off back to the same door. They were still looking at me because there is no time in these dimensions. I presented the papers and told them I was cutting that trade-off of my family. I shut the door and broke it off my family line. When I woke up the next morning after doing this it felt like a monkey had been taken off my back. Something that had always been with me was gone.

The four faces of the commanded blessing of Yahweh can be placed on the cube. These four faces are found in Scripture and are called the good, acceptable, perfect and commanded blessings.

   - The good blessing corresponds to the thirty-fold increase.
   - The acceptable blessing corresponds to the sixty-fold increase.
   - The perfect blessing corresponds to the hundred-fold increase.

These are our developmental stages as we mature in the Kingdom:

   - The good blessing represents the slave.
   - The acceptable blessing represents the servant.
   - The perfect blessing represents stewards.
   - The commanded blessing is sonship

The last one to develop is the commanded blessing of Yahweh and relates to finances and how we, as sons, grow into maturity. When we first got saved, we started to tithe. Then we gave gifts. When we get to the 'perfect blessing' stage we start to do leverage trades and the giving of *terumah* which is the giving of our first fruit. A commanded blessing comes upon a son who works through all of these areas into a never-ending supply because that son says, "Yahweh, it's all Yours. Tell me what I can keep and I give the rest to whichever cause needs it." In the Church Age this last stage was the 'you must know the will of God for your life' stage.

When I got born again from above, I started to operate in the 'good' will of Yahweh. I tithed, I was a good person and I wanted to learn to obey God and to do what He told me to. As I started to mature, I began to understand the 'acceptable' will of God for my life, which was the 60-fold blessing, and I started giving more than just my tithe. I started operating in the manner of a servant and wanted to do whatever I could in church. As I matured further, I began to operate in the 'perfect' will of God, which was the hundred-fold and I became a steward of what He wanted for me. I began to do gifts and giving, leverage and *terumah*. I've been giving *terumah* for twenty years. The commanded blessings started to follow me as I began to operate as a son in the Kingdom and I engaged in the four faces of the 'commanded' blessing of Yahweh. Each one was a door and each door led into the next one.

We are sons, building the 13th Age. We are also sons in the 13th Priesthood being revealed for the sake of all of creation which is groaning and waiting for us to manifest. We are sons, in the 13th Age, building a New Heaven and a New Earth. Our job as a priest is to administrate our Father into creation and not administrating creation to the Father. Again, this is a cube which sits within us, so when we administrate His name and say the *Yod, Hey, Vav, Hey*, we are creating an echo chamber of His name and who He is, within us. This is what it means to be a priest of our Father.

When we say the *Yod, Hey, Vav, Hey*, we can say that the *Yod* represents the Word, *Hey* is life, the *Vav* is light and the last *Hey* is love. These are not the actual meanings of the Hebrew letters but representations. When we say the *Yod, Hey, Vav, Hey*, we are releasing the Word, His life, His light and His love, as a priest of our Father, into the cube that sits within us. When we stand in the middle of His name, we are creating an echo chamber of His name around us and we are administrating our Father into creation.

Praying in the Spirit administrates the priesthood of Yahweh within us and we also begin to release the Word, life, light and love through the names of who He is. The *Yod, Hey, Vav, Hey* is a mystery which the Jews have kept hidden, but speaking in tongues is a secret and was only released in the book of Acts. When you speak in tongues, you build yourself up in your most holy faith, by releasing the four-pillared exchange of His name within you, and releasing His Word, His life, His light and His love, as a priest of Yahweh. Tongues pre-dates *Genesis 1:1* because before Yahweh created letters He created a Heavenly language. He then created the Living Letters with which He created creation. Speaking in tongues is vitally important for us to do and it's not old fashioned! We are allowed to use our sanctified imagination when we first start engaging because our imagination is an ancient door through which we can enter into an actual encounter - where we don't imagine any more because it becomes a reality. The Word says in *2 Corinthians 10:5* that we must take captive every thought and bring it into submission to Christ, so I find it helpful to put my fingers in my ears and all

I can hear is myself speaking in tongues. This keeps my mind from wandering.

Once, I was on a long car trip and I was engaging with His name, saying the *Yod, Hey, Vav, Hey* over and over. After a while, I heard a clicking within me, like the cogs of a wheel clicking into place inside of me and I began to ascend out of the vehicle WITH my body. There's something unbelievably powerful about understanding the four-pillared exchange of His name and the echo chamber of His name.

Chapter 5
Faith - Part One

I was born again into the Word of Faith movement so the concept of faith was a solid foundation in my life. My husband also knew Faith, as does my daughter. When she first met the Being of Faith, she told me that she had always known him because he had always been around her father. I had so much confidence in his ability to hear from God because whatever he said was going to happen, did.

In the Hebrew language, objects have genders. In the Greek way of thinking mostly everything is an 'it'. A good way of finding out if something is male or female is to use the interlinear feature of the Blue Letter Bible. My whole Christian life was spent walking by faith and living by faith but when I actually met the Being of Faith it was a completely new journey for me. My husband was taught that faith was a force so he did not have the language to describe his relationship with Faith, but he did understand the concept of faith. When he was diagnosed with cancer he, by faith, worshipped his way to divine health without taking the treatment as taking it had made him very ill. When he passed away, it wasn't through sickness, it was because his scroll was finished and he had the faith to transition.

The pivotal Scripture in the New Testament regarding faith is *Hebrews 11:1*, "Now faith is the substance of things hoped for, the evidence of things not seen." The Word of Faith movement built their whole theology on this truth. In the Old Testament the word 'trust' is used in place of 'faith' so the two words serve the same purpose. *Proverbs 3:5* says, "Trust in the LORD with all your heart, and lean not on your own understanding; in all your ways acknowledge Him, and He shall direct your paths." In Hebrew, the word 'trust' is *betach*, written with a *Beit*, *Tet* and *Chet*. When we look up what these Living Letters mean we can read it as follows: trust is like a wall surrounding the house of your belief system. The word 'acknowledge' means to engage someone as a partner in what you are doing and 'heart' refers to your inner man. Thus, we can read the Scripture as follows: Trust is like a wall, surrounding the house of your belief system, within your inner man, engaging Him as a partner in what you are doing. Our mindset aligns itself with our positioning, so if we're thinking incorrectly within this mystical movement then we are not positioned well. We must go above the sun, by faith, allowing faith to wall us in and pull us in so we find ourselves engaging with Him as a partner in order to be positioned well so we can begin to walk in that path.

Some people have great encounters when they get born again but others have to do it by faith. When we go through life, we need to do it by faith without relying on encounters to validate it. Angels don't come to us and introduce themselves as our angel; they wait for us to acknowledge their existence. Many of us have seen a sudden flash of light or we've seen something move in our peripheral vision. These angels are waiting for us to turn towards them, introduce ourselves and engage with them; when that happens, they will be more approachable and start to interact with us. We engage with them by faith.

Sons who are well positioned, can now walk in the fullness of maturity. We're building a legacy so we can walk into the season of Goshen that is ahead of us. Many things happened in the world during 2023; difficult economic times, governmental issues, wars and rumours of wars and pestilences amongst others. Even so, we've landed a structure called the 13th Tribe.

Moses built the 12 pillars under the mountain and built an altar there which represents the 13th Tribe. This tribe was a secret one and not spoken of – it represented Dinah. We are now that Tribe, doing what was written in *Joel 2:7-9*, "They run like mighty men, they climb the wall like men of war; every one marches in formation, and they do not break ranks. They do not push one another; every one marches in his own column. Though they lunge between the weapons, they are not cut down. They run to and fro in the city, they run on the wall; they climb into the houses, they enter at the windows like a thief." In that same chapter Scripture says that He will turn the sun and moon back to look at the faces of Yahweh and bring them back to their original intent because they are currently in their fallen estate. It has nothing to do with a blood moon.

At the time of writing, we were in the process of navigating a global recession, which is always the aftermath of any kind of world-wide pandemic or war. We have the choice to get depressed about it or we can position ourselves above the sun because when we do that, the things happening in the world do not touch us. We know the story of those who lived in the land of Goshen in Egypt but now we can't just re-tell the story, we have to start living there ourselves. We do that by living above the sun within the atmosphere of the frequency of Goshen.

Crazy things have been happening to me because faith has garrisoned itself like a wall, surrounding my belief system in my inner man which helps me to engage with Him as a partner in all that I do. Faith becomes the evidence of things not seen but that which I've been trusting for. I found the door of full supply - I've read the story of the widow's oil many times without really understanding it but now I'm constantly aware of being positioned within this doorway as I close it upon myself.

When I was in the process of applying for my UK citizenship I began to engage with Faith because it's the substance of things hoped for and the evidence of things not seen. By faith I was blessing and honouring the Being of Faith while I was on my way to get my document, however, there were a few discrepancies in my paperwork. As I was doing this, I saw the Being of Faith walk towards me in the spirit and so I started to engage with the Law of Faith and I saw them come together and form an arc over me. I then saw what looked like a red carpet rolling out in front of them. It was favour. By a miracle, I received my citizenship that day.

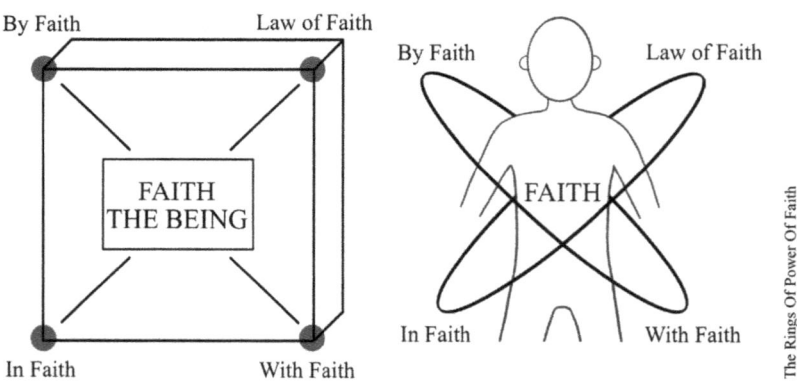

Faith works together with other pillars. One such pillar is Honour which seals, protects and expands what Faith brings towards us. The Being of Faith and the Being of Honour stand on either side of us like pillars and form an archway. There is always a pathway that leads through these pillars which is called *haDerech* or The Way. Jesus said, "I am *haDerech*." In Proverbs, Wisdom says, "I stand in the way." Similarly, the pillar of Faith and the pillar of the Law of Faith arc together and the path leads through them. *Romans 10:17* says, "So faith comes from hearing, and hearing through the word of Christ." As these two Beings arc, faith becomes the substance of things hoped for and as we walk on that pathway it becomes the evidence of things not yet seen and manifests itself. Faith is a belief and a firm persuasion; it is the assurance and the conviction of something. If we have faith, then nothing will turn us away from our belief structure, no matter what.

I firmly believe that any economic crisis will not affect me because I have positioned myself above the sun. One morning I woke up feeling that everything was well with my life when suddenly I saw the trajectory of my life taking a downturn. When I enquired of the Lord what that meant He told me that that was my future and that I was coming to the end of my life in the years to come. As a woman of faith, that has walked this path for over 40 years, that came as a shock to me. He then told me that I was still sitting under the sun. That statement set me on a mission to finding out what that path looked like.

I'm far too fond of conspiracy theories which is why I don't engage with them. During COVID, I was in South Africa for two years and endured a lot of criticism because I took the inoculation. I complained to the Lord about the worldwide pandemic and asked Him when He was going to do something about it. He looked at me and asked me what it had to do with me. I then realized that if I'm living above the sun then it has nothing to do with me. Nothing anyone did change the fact that COVID was happening. No amount of social media posts or petitions changed it. If we continue to prophesy under the sun, then it will always be from a negative aspect. There are many prophets in today's world who have the truth but because they're operating from under a star system, under the sun, they cannot see what is above it and prophesy like the prophets of old did.

I know a lady whose dad was an orphan. The government

of that country used to inject these children and conducted experiments on them. Her dad used to often be ill because of those injections. When Hitler rose to power his regime did the same thing. They performed experiments in the concentration camps. Many of the medicines we take today are the result of experiments that took place in Auschwitz. There are cancer patients who are undergoing treatments free of charge because they are being experimented on with trial medication. In the case of COVID, the whole world was included in this trial, mostly without permission, which became an issue.

This has happened in the past and it will happen again – it seems that there is nothing we can do about it even if we legislate, however Yahweh used the time of COVID to teach us many things and to shift us into something new. When I was asked when I was going to address the issue of the injections I said, "There is no issue because we have always been experimented on." When I took the injection (I took it above the sun so speak) it didn't give me any side effects whatsoever. I took the second injection and when it tried to manifest, I told it to move along and stop its nonsense. I walked with Faith when I had my two inoculations because *Mark 16:18* says, "They will take up serpents; and if they drink anything deadly, it will by no means hurt them; they will lay hands on the sick, and they will recover." If the Father tells me that something needs to be done, then I will go ahead and engage with it. If not, then I will be aware of it, however will not deal into it. A prophetic person should be reading a person's scroll but many prophets bring 'words' that they have picked up from the familiar spirits around a person's life and are giving words of knowledge rather than looking to that person's future. Once we start living above the sun, and we eat our scroll, it starts to speak from within us and we can see what our future holds.

Confirmation Bias is a psychological term which means that we look for things that can feed and confirm our bias. We discard what doesn't fit into it and run after that which does. In the context of COVID we could say that we believe the injection is bad and that it kills people. We will gather all the articles and information we can which confirms what we believe. However, when we go above the sun, we can ask the Father to help us to not just hear what suits our nativity or the way we were raised. When we live above the sun we can learn from all sorts of teachings as long as we learn how to filter them. I was taught a good lesson by the Father; I had seen a dragon come out of a mountain in a certain country and I started to legislate together with a group of others. A huge disaster was averted. When the dragon left that mountain and entered into another one in South America, I immediately went after it. I clearly heard the Father tell me to stop it as this one had nothing to do with me. I argued with Him because of the disaster it would cause to that country but I was clearly told not to interfere because it was none of my business to be there at that time. Through that, I learned to only do what I see the Father doing, just like Yeshua Himself said.

I now call people to come above the sun with me so that I can teach them how to be kings and priests so that they can put it into practice in the areas they live in to affect local government and the community at large. We can do this because we have come from a secret place. I recently met with some folk to ask them how they were doing as I couldn't feel them in my heart anymore. Their excuse was that they had been busy. I knew that wasn't the true reason but I gave them the benefit of the doubt. Two weeks later, they called me to set up an appointment to see me. When we sat down, I said that I would tell them why they had come to see me, where they were going and why they had made that decision. They could then tell me if I was right or wrong. I was right and that is how the prophetic should work. We can do this with nations too.

By the Spirit of the Lord, I'm saying to shore up your finances, don't spend it on silly things and learn to live in the land of Goshen. Find the place of full supply because we're going into a season of strange things happening globally. Joseph prepared for seven years in order to survive the seven lean years and the grain that had been stored was still fresh. How did that happen? He had discovered a technology and had become a fountain to the people around him. He lived above the sun which is where he had all his encounters which we've interpreted as being his dreams. The reason I can teach on the widow's oil that didn't run out is because I've found myself in the same place she was in. She found oil while I found meat. I was able to feed 120 families for a period of time and every time I took some meat out the deep freeze it would be replaced. Rick and I bought a deep freeze for a lady in Uganda who looks after children in an orphanage. I asked her how it was coping with their frequent power cuts and she replied that she had instructed her deep freeze to behave like mine and it stayed cold through all the power cuts. She told me that it never defrosts and is always full of meat. We cannot say that we cannot give because we have no money; that is totally against what the Scriptures teach us. The only way to stop the devourer is to give. I'm so thankful for every disaster we have had because I've been able to take them and turn them into a love story. I love this demonstration of faith. As a widow, I run two households in two different countries as well as looking after my frail father.

We've recently endured the worst floods in 100 years. The Lord showed me prophetically that it was coming but I didn't do anything about it. After the floods we were without water for 17 days and we were able to raise enough money to install water tanks for 10 families so that they would never have to be without water again. I want to take every bad thing and make it work for me because I've understood how to arc with the Being of Faith and the Law of Faith. I have an intimate relationship with them and only do what the Father tells me to do and it always works. It might tarry but it always happens.

We walk with the Being of Faith and the Law of Faith and do things by faith, in faith and through faith. Ian Clayton uses the phrase "Rings of Power", which I equate to the cube; so if the Being of Faith is in the centre of the cube then I engage by faith, with the law of faith, with faith and in faith which are all pillars of the Being of Faith. Likewise, we can place this within ourselves, with the Being of Faith placed inside of us and the four pillars placed on each shoulder and each foot which create rings of power that oscillate within who we are. We know that without faith it is impossible to please God.

The 12 laws of Jerusalem govern who we are, as people, and even though we are in a new age they do still apply because they're written in Scripture.

- The law of sowing and reaping – even if someone is not a Christian, it works, because it's a law. Nature observes this law like it observes the law of gravity. *Galatians 6:8-9.*
- The law of sin and death - *Romans 8:1.*
- The law of the Spirit of life in Christ Jesus - *Romans 8:2.*
- The law of love - *Mark 12:3.*
- The law of first mention. An example of this is where the fig tree is spoken to by Jesus and He tells it that the next day it would be dead. The first time a fig tree was mentioned is in the Garden when the glory was gone from Adam and Eve and they covered themselves with the leaves of the fig tree. According to Hebrew understanding, the fig tree implies that it covered

the glory. It was supposed to be producing fruit and it wasn't so Jesus just said, "Tomorrow you'll be dead because nothing covers the glory."

- The law of abundance - *Matthew 13:12.*
- The law of justice – this is what underpins a prophetic person because they want to see justice done. The prophets of old wanted justice for God and for righteousness. People with a prophetic nature need to govern their need for justice which is why it's so important to be above the sun. The need for justice can supersede what Yahweh is saying.
- The law of righteousness - *Romans 6:14.*
- The law of judgement. *Matthew 7:2.*
- The law of grace. *Romans 6:14.*
- The law of mercy. *Matthew 5:7.*
- The law of faith - *Romans 3:27.*

Laws are put in place to govern and can only be superseded if there is a higher law. In *Romans 8:1* we read about the law of sin and death which is superseded by the next law in verse 2 which is the law of the Spirit of life in Christ Jesus. John G. Lake, a man of great faith, came to South Africa as a missionary in the early 20th century. There had been an outbreak of the Bubonic plague and he and his assistant were helping the medical corps to carry the victims from their homes. This plague was extremely contagious so that even after death, the germs could kill a healthy individual who touched the dead body. When the doctors questioned him and asked why he was not affected by the germs he replied that he believed in the living God and His power. He did an experiment with the doctors; they placed the foam of a victim's lungs in his hands, put it under a microscope and watched the live contagious germs die instantly. He then said, "The Law of the Spirit of Life in Christ Jesus has set me free from the Law of Sin and Death. I believe that just as long as I keep my soul in contact with the living God so that His Spirit is flowing into my soul and body, that no germ will ever attach itself to me, for the Spirit of God will kill it." (www.healingrooms.com; The Law of Life and the Law of Death by John G. Lake). He was possessed by the law of the Spirit of life in Christ Jesus and was firmly positioned above the Sun.

The twelve laws don't demand our attention; they want our wilful obedience so that they can become rings of power within us and work with us so that we can start to step out in faith within this 13th Age. These laws also release a sense of engagement which can only come out of relationship. I understood that there was a law of faith so as I began to engage with Faith and then through Faith, arc with the law of faith, favour was released. In order for these laws to operate in our lives we have to acknowledge them. John G. Lake acknowledged the law when he said that he was possessed by the law of the Spirit of life in Christ Jesus. These laws were in place before God created creation. Mountains are places of government that we can place these twelve laws upon. Each of these mountains have a governing seat which Yahweh established before creation. We are able to take our seat on these governing mountains, through a relationship with faith, and we can rule as kings in the realm of who we are and what we do. Each of these laws carry power and John G. Lake clearly understood that sitting on this seat of the governing power of the law of the Spirit of life in Christ Jesus meant that nothing could touch him. Things can be really bad in the world, so this message of faith is good because we need to know how to live by faith in the land of Goshen which is the place of full supply! These laws govern us to establish a way of life to flow through us. But, we cannot operate in them if we are not above the sun. I engaged with the Being of Faith, by faith, until the substance of what Faith looked like manifested right in front of me.

Many years ago I found out, through a friend, that Honour is a Being. I was leading a group of people through two pillars, one of which was the pillar of honour, when I suddenly saw two pillars standing on either side of me. They were huge, and so was I. I watched myself on the earth, walking with this group of people on *haDerech*, and I was wondering who I was, if I was also on the earth walking through the process. I realized that I was an illuminary/illumination seeing myself walking this road by faith. Honour then came towards me and I introduced myself to him. The next day a friend contacted me to say that Honour had told him that we had met the previous day and he wanted to say hello to me! It is incredibly important for us to engage in these realms, by faith.

We might be wondering if what we're believing for is from the Father. Either He puts the desire into our hearts or we do. If it doesn't come to pass we just need to try again. If we're above the sun, and we engage into something that the Father has told us to do, it will always come to pass. We are stepping into this Age to learn what it looks like to see the overshadowing hand of Yahweh. We have become the ceiling for creation where it can only do as much as we allow it to do. Creation is groaning and waiting for the manifestation of the glory of the sons of God. If it's still groaning it means we haven't yet done our part. We are in partnership with plants because we breathe in the oxygen which the plant releases and the plant breathes in carbon dioxide which we breathe out. In effect, we are the other part of its lung and we work together in a synergistic relationship.

In *Genesis 1,* God spoke and things came into being. When He made the earth, He told the earth to bring forth fruit-bearing trees and it did. He didn't make the trees; He told creation to make them and the land produced. The ability to create is invested in creation so, Like Yahweh did, we must speak to the land and tell it to produce. We do this by faith, in faith, through faith, by the law of faith as we become the full expression of the 13th Tribe.

I heard a clinical psychologist say that although carbon emissions are a global problem, there has been an increase in rainfall world-wide which has caused plants to grow and plants absorb carbon emissions. He has also reported that as a result of all the rain, the deserts are shrinking. I recently watched the Paris to Dakar race and for the first time ever I saw trucks getting stuck in mud – in the desert. Creation knows how to heal itself. When we were in hard lockdown, due to COVID, we could all see how creation responded to the lack of human interference. Fish reappeared in previously polluted bodies of water; the air cleared and everything looked better. The Father had given creation a one-word command; to produce. And it did.

Yahweh has told me a number of times to start kindergartens in the poorest areas of town. All my Kindergartens were started without money, by faith. These children were given two meals a day as well as good quality primary education in fully equipped classrooms. Even when the parents could not afford the minimal school fees we never struggled to make ends meet because I understood the journey of faith. I used to be a missionary and after my husband transitioned I would have never been able to run a church without knowing who Faith was. I used to remind Yahweh of the Scripture that says, "I will never let the righteous go hungry or their seed begging for bread." *Proverbs 37:25.*

I have a Patreon page and some of the money I receive from that forum is used to look after two small children who were abandoned. Both had been malnourished and had severe internal issues because of it. The lady who is looking after them told me that she had some bloodwork done on the children and one of them came back HIV positive. I spent some time chatting to her explaining that through good nutrition, love, positive touch and Yeshua, his status would change from HIV positive to HIV negative. Those on my Patreon page joined me in engaging on behalf of that child. A while later I received another report from bloodwork done. He was HIV negative.

I was radically born again from above when I was 17 years old. I was getting ready to go to a School Prefect's Prom when I heard a voice in my right ear say to me, "I don't want you to go to Teacher's Training College, I want you to go to Bible school." I replied, "Father, I will do it as long as You promise I am never without work and money and I don't have to struggle." The hard times have come but they are good for us because the Bible says that He woos us into the wilderness so He can show us the door of hope. The only place where we can eat at a table of plenty is in the presence of our enemy. We have to learn how to walk with pain and grief because it creates a platform for us to step on which brings us to the next level. These are building blocks to bring us to maturity.

Should another pandemic arise we need to have learned from the previous one so we don't repeat the same mistakes. I do believe that Yahweh used COVID to take us into a place of rest but I also think that it could have been for a shorter period of time if we had been able to come into agreement and walk in unity instead of fighting against one another. We are going to have to learn how to step into the Nano world, past the Sea of Everything and past the Realm of Nothingness. One of our guest speakers was at one of our yearly intensives when he saw a vortex open, and there were four more races of angelic Beings within that realm. Their prime purpose is to guard the throne of Yahweh. They are the *Hashmallim*, the *Ophenim*, the *Chayot haKodesh* and the *Erelim* and are there to serve in the Father's house and to bring us into our full inheritance. They are placed above the *Seraphim* and guard the *Shekinah* who created a canopy for the throne of Yahweh so He could begin to speak into creation. It seems like there is a whole other world that we know nothing about. I'm not sure that there is a Scripture for that place but I do know that Scripture is a living, breathing entity which only reveals its secrets when we are ready to receive it, so it's possible that that Scripture exists; we just haven't seen it yet.

God chooses to not know certain things because He holds the will of man as a very precious thing. If He did choose to know everything then we would all just be puppets on a string. I disagree with those who say that He will force everyone to come into His sovereign will. What is the point of walking the narrow road and keeping ourselves holy if everyone will serve Him in the end anyway? He gives us the right, by faith, to choose as He gave the angelic realm the right to choose. Lucifer chose his path and God let him take it; He didn't stop the choice.

The Jews say that God is an ever-expanding horizon, with the upper waters within Him feeding the lower waters within Him, which sets a platform for Him to keep creating. He is an evolutionary learning Being. Does God just have one will for our lives or are there many for us to choose from? He hopes that we choose at least one because He holds our will as sacrosanct. When we say, "I'll just leave it in God's hands," what are we saying? Hands are not meant just for holding but to cover and govern which means that we're abdicating our position. We're meant to do it, not Him. He is entrusting the restoration of the earth and the creation of a New Heaven and a New Earth to us.

Our engagement with Faith unlocks the law of Faith in us. The glory of God needs to rest on something that looks like itself. If there is no faith, then He can't. Faith and the law of Faith arc together to form a window called the Glory of God which establishes itself over us. When the people congregated in the tabernacle the priest would bless them and sing the *Yod Hey Vav Hey* over them which opened up portals of glory which in turn opened up dimensions. *Shekinah* covered the packed tabernacle, where there was standing room only, and the people would all fall down. This was called the miracle of the Tabernacle – the tabernacle would expand to allow the people to have space so they would not be lying on top of each other.

When the glory lifted, they would stand up and the tabernacle would shrink to its original dimensions. That makes the tabernacle itself a living entity. This is a type and shadow because He now lives in us and we are living entities.

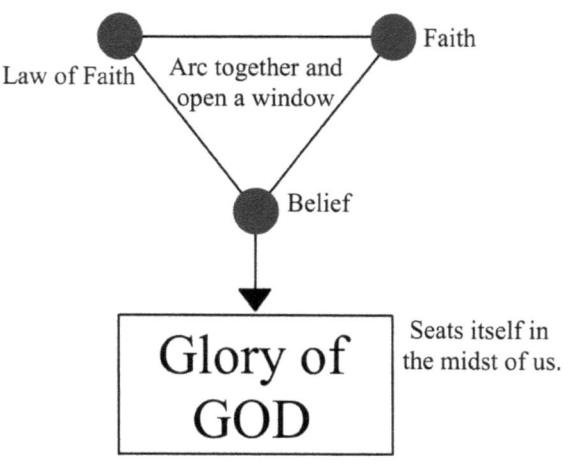

The arcing of the law of faith/being of faith/belief

Chapter 6
Faith - Part Two

In *Psalm 91:5* we read, "You shall not be afraid of the terror by night, nor of the arrow that flies by day." In my experience the sole purpose of the terror by night is to shut down our sight through fear. Most small children see things that frighten them, especially when they're supposed to be sleeping.

My daughter didn't have night terrors but my two sons and my foster child did. The night terror frightens the child to such an extent that they shut out the good with the bad and refuse to 'see' anymore. I have met many adults (mostly women) who cannot sleep at night without a night light burning somewhere because they are afraid of the dark. They have not dealt with the terror by night and still fear it. The only way to deal with it is to sit in the dark and when it comes towards you, you have to address it and tell it that it has no hold over you and it has to leave. It's that simple. It doesn't argue with you, it just leaves. However, if we don't deal with it we won't see the angelic realm when it appears because we'll be so used to shutting down anything from another realm. **Monsters Inc.** was a popular children's animated movie which demonstrated exactly how night terrors work. The monsters accessed the child's room through a special door and had to scare the child so that it screamed in terror. That fear then fed the monsters' realm so that they could continue to exist. From very little I was able to clearly see into the demonic realm until I shut it down 10 years ago.

My uncle, my cousin and my mother were all born with the caul and they had a sixth sense which meant they could all easily see or sense things that others couldn't. It is said that being born with the caul opens up the third eye. My mother was born to be a psychic or a medium but because she was brought up in the Anglican church, she was extremely uncomfortable with that aspect of her nature. She could see and was a prophet without being born again! My great great-uncle was a white witch – he said it was better than a black witch – and used to entertain party guests by levitating tables. When I was born again I could immediately see the demonic realm but not the angelic because the church taught us we were not allowed to interact with angels in case we were deceived.

After 30 years, I got so bored of dealing with the demonic and the alien realm that I told the Lord I didn't want to see the demonic realm anymore; He defeated that realm 2000 years ago so why was I still fighting the enemy? I do still occasionally do deliverance with people who cannot get rid of the strongholds themselves and I do believe that there are demons in this world but I don't have demons hovering over my home or coming into my room anymore. On occasion a witch will come past on a ley line but then I just cover it with the blood of the Lamb and shut it down so they can't use that path anymore. I've also learned how to place my mountain over my house so I don't even get visited by astral projectors anymore. I've had to train myself to see the Godly things and how to respond to them without panicking.

When I had an encounter with Mary and Joseph my first response was: I'm not catholic; why are they coming to talk to me? She was lovely and she told me that she always knew that she would be the one to carry the Messiah because she wanted to fulfil her chosen scroll. Her childless parents would go to the temple regularly to pray for a child until they fell pregnant with her and when she was weaned she was dedicated to temple service as was the custom. I was allowed to see a photograph that was taken in Jerusalem of a painting which shows the priests making a sacrifice and behind them is a little serving girl – Mary. When Jesus was born, Simeon and Anna both said that they could die knowing that they had seen the Messiah. They both knew Mary because they had served in the temple together. Joseph then told me that he knew that Mary was carrying the Messiah after the angel announced it to him. I was in such a hurry to leave that encounter that I realized too late that Mary was handing me something. I had to go back to that encounter where she was still waiting, because there is no time in that realm.

My response has always been to run away from these spiritual encounters and I've had to train myself to stand my ground. I was in New Zealand, at one of Ian's conferences, when Enoch appeared beside me. I asked Ian what I should do and he said I should introduce myself to him but I was too frightened. The next day Enoch walked towards me and instead of introducing myself and greeting him I stared at his beard. It looked like moving mercury and when I looked into his eyes, I could see whole universes in them. At this point, I ran away again. On the third attempt I was able to introduce myself and he spoke with me. I've had to train myself to turn off seeing so vividly in the demonic realm and, by faith, open the door to the other realm and respond in a godly manner. The terror by night created this trigger in me and I've had to learn how to overcome it.We're learning to see Faith as a Being and if we're avoiding our triggers and not dealing with what we're seeing then we will never engage with Faith.

Ricky had an encounter with the Spirit of Understanding who told him that the people had a lot of knowledge but needed to have understanding. On one occasion the Lion of the tribe of

Judah came into my house, bowed down before me and asked me what he could do for me. I had handed the church over to Ricky and Melanie, and they were needing some assistance so I asked him if he would go and help them. I then phoned Melanie to tell her what had happened and she replied that she had seen the Lion of Judah a few times before and he would go and help them when they needed assistance. I know that demons exist but I don't interact with them anymore and I choose to not feed them. I've seen them grow through feeding on a person's fear. The opposite is also true; when we turn our attention, by faith, to the angelic realm then they are attracted to us and we are able to interact with them.

In *Hebrews 10:25* we read, "… not forsaking the assembling of ourselves together, as is the manner of some, but exhorting one another, and so much the more as you see the Day." Many in the religious church quote that Scripture to prove that we should meet regularly i.e. on a Sunday and as a pastor I used it for years to justify why we met every week. When was the 'the Day' first mentioned? The law of first mention is powerful and the first time this was used was in *Genesis 2:4* where Scripture says, "This is the history of the Heavens and the earth when they were created, in the day that the Lord God made the earth and the Heavens …" That 'Day' was a whole different creation so if I look at the Scripture in *Hebrews 10:25,* I can look at 'The Day' and see a dimensional shift. We're literally sitting in the middle of the shifting into the 13th Age within Goshen. We're not in the end times but we are in the middle of the change of an Age. The religious system does not want to be friends with us if we don't believe what they believe. We could have fellowship because we all love Jesus, but it doesn't work which is why we have Hub gatherings all over the world so we can have community.

We cannot live above the sun if we don't understand Faith and in the next few years it will become vital for us to be able to do this. During COVID, I refused to listen to all the talk regarding the pros and cons of taking the injection and I was highly criticized because of my stance but I only wanted to hear what the Father had to say about it. He told me it had nothing to do with me and He chose to reset the entire globe by using the pandemic to His advantage. We must be careful not to make gods according to the idols in our own heart. God cannot and will not go against His Word so we cannot say that God told us something is alright for us to do when it clearly isn't.

Prophets were not always just there to see the future, they prophesied because they wanted justice in a situation or in the land. There are many prophetic people in this mystical movement and because we want to see justice, we swoop under the sun and the star system, with the balancing scales of Libra, and we start to judge like they did in the Old Testament. What we should be doing is go above the sun and ask the Father IF we should be doing something. If He says nothing, then we should do nothing. We'll know when we are above the sun because it's very quiet there. There is no clamour of voices telling us that everything is out to get us. The Jews were living in Egypt under terrible conditions but they were living in Goshen so when the plagues were sent they had no symptoms at all. We have a choice; are we going to read that as a story or are we going to live like we are in the land of Goshen? Ian has noticed that those living under the sun are under tremendous economic pressure but it doesn't seem to touch those who are living above the sun because Yahweh makes a way where there seems to be no way. We know that our faith level has moved when we start to feel fearful. When we engage under the sun and we're not in union with Faith we start to engage with Libra and the judging scales, but we can always move back above the sun and ask the

Father what He is saying.

When we walk with Faith, in Faith, by Faith and with the law of Faith they arc together to create *haDerech* where the Being of Favour can follow us and operate with us. I've learned how to pull time towards me and how to change and shift it. I never say that I've run out of time, or that time is money, or don't waste time, because we say those things when we are positioned under the sun. Time as we know it does not exist above the sun; Time is a beautiful and honourable Being. I had to take my son and his family to Gatwick airport and the traffic was particularly heavy that morning. The longer we were driving, the longer the GPS said it would take us to get there so I was engaging with Time as I wanted to be at the airport by 09:00am. We eventually arrived at 09:35am and after dropping my family at departures I made my way home. I was feeling rather unhappy with the delay, when I received a message from my son saying that they were having breakfast before getting on their flight. They had gone through passport control, customs and check in, with a baby and luggage, in 20 minutes! Time then said, "I did what you asked me to do but not in the way that you expected." I learned a valuable lesson right there.

Everything that Yahweh does starts in the Spirit realm first and then it begins to manifest itself in the natural realm. Our physical body is firstly spiritual because it is divine. We must learn how to walk through walls and translocate because our physical body has a technology within it. The only problem we have with walking through a wall is in our head. I was lying in bed one night and listening to Ian teaching about walking through walls. I put my hand out to touch the wall and it kept on going through; I could feel the cavity inside the wall and the rough texture of the stone and brick. I was shocked and immediately pulled my hand back for fear that it would be stuck inside the wall. After that incident, I would stick coins to the wall (without glue). Whenever we had meetings with a group of New Age folk, they would practice sticking coins to the wall, not to show how spiritual they were, but because it was an issue of frequency. Thereafter we had gold and silver dust and nuggets appearing in our meetings along with bubbles and feathers. The New Agers love and honour the angelic realm and see angels all the time but are not very interested in Jesus. As a demonstration of faith, I showed them how to stick coins to the wall. How are we going to walk through matter or become invisible or translocate? We must first understand how to step into it by Faith, in Faith and through Faith.

Quantum physics teaches us that matter has memory and is a living entity. My house knows my intention but it also knows that I need it to stay upright and keep the weather out and the warmth in. *The Double-Slit Experiment shows how particles of light behave. When the particles are watched they do what they are supposed to do but when they are not watched they behave haphazardly. Scientists came to the conclusion that matter knows when it is being observed. Why did Jesus not knock on the locked door when He visited His disciples after His resurrection? He wanted to show us something by walking through the wall and I believe we will be able to do the same. When I moved to England and handed the South African church over to Rick and Mel I would sing and worship while I was waiting to start my own meeting in the UK as I was 2 hours behind South Africa. They would contact me to say they could hear my voice over the monitors! One of the ladies in my group told me she knows when I'm there because she can smell my perfume. Recently I woke up in the middle of the night and I could hear someone talking. I got up to check what was happening but everyone and everything was still fast asleep. The next day a friend contacted me to tell me she had been praying for me in the early hours of the morning and that's what I could

* this experiment can be found on Youtube

hear when I woke up. These things happen by Faith, in Faith and through Faith, not because we are special but because we walk together in a relationship.

The physical world always has a connection into heaven and the Word and the Living Letters are the doorway through which our Father's Kingdom begins to present itself. This is why faith comes by hearing and hearing by the Word of God. We must be purposeful in our engagement with Faith because Faith is the connector between these two realms. We become purposeful by:

- Praying in the Spirit.
- Drawing on a memory of what has happened and building a record on that memory. Hebrews 11 does exactly that, to encourage folk that it can be done again. When we share a testimony we are declaring that God can do it again. If He provided for us once, why can He not do it again?
- Focusing on a section of Scripture. I like to use the interlinear feature of the Blue Letter Bible because I enjoy looking at the original intent of words.

I was listening to Wisdom's Echo where a friend of mine was teaching on the Disciple's Prayer. We've often read the Scripture that says: give us this day our daily bread and we've understood it to mean our daily provision. When we look at the law of first mention we see that the priests in the temple would take their three-pronged fork, that looked like a *Shin*, thrust it into the pot where the offering had been placed and pull out their supply of meat for the day. It also means getting our daily supply of the secrets of Yahweh. The Greek translation says it's the supply of bread for tomorrow. When we pray we can ask the Father to give us our provision and the revelation of the secrets and mysteries for today and tomorrow. This is why the Word is important because it gives us something to hold on to.

Genesis 1:3 says, "And God said, 'Let there be light,' and there was." In *Genesis 1:4* we read, "And God saw the light, that it was good; and God divided the light from the darkness." In *Genesis 1:5* it continues, "God called the light Day, and the darkness He called Night. So the evening and the morning were the first day." We see from these Scriptures that God said it, God saw it and God called it which leads us to *Hebrews 11:1* – faith is the substance of things hoped for; the evidence of things not yet seen. We say it by faith, we see the substance of it by faith and we call the evidence of faith into being. When we live above the sun we will know what we need to call into being because the Father will tell us. Many people pray for change in their respective country's government but we must remember that people get the government they deserve according to what is in their hearts. We also get non-productive governments if we do not govern correctly ourselves. We need radically born-again people, from all walks of life, operating within their spheres of influence, whether it be politics, Hollywood, business and the like.

We can only build something in the realms of the Kingdom if we can see it which is why we say it, we see it and then we call it in – Faith, Substance, Evidence. Substance is the reality of what we want to see happen. There is potential in everything. I love my plants and speak to them all the time. I had a lovely tomato plant which I spoke to and told it to produce fruit. It gave me three harvests. When winter came I put the plant behind the garage so I could dispose of it the following spring and then forgot about it. One day, during winter, I had to get something from the garage and saw the discarded tomato plant – without a single leaf but full of tomatoes! It spoke to me and said, "You never told me to stop producing." I apologized to my plant, picked the fruit and told it to stop producing. The following day it was dead.

Hope ignites the fire and belief within us where the Pillar of Hope and the Pillar of Faith arc together and then the evidence manifests itself on earth. Hope deferred makes the heart sick, *Proverbs 13:12*, but when we have hope, igniting fire and belief by faith, evidence begins to manifest. The dictionary definition of 'substance' is: a particular form of matter with uniform properties - the real physical matter of which a person or thing consists and which has a tangible, solid presence. In Greek it means foundation and steadfastness of mind. When I say it, see it and call it, it creates substance which is the foundation of who I am – this is how we will create a New Heaven and a New Earth. We cannot say that we have done things like moving star systems or tectonic plates and then not see physical evidence of it somewhere. There has to be a news article or some sort of media release reporting an unusual event.

Faith is a Being but it is also a realm that we can enter and drink from. The Hebrew word that gets translated 'faith' is the word 'belief' or אמונה *emunah*. The Seven Spirits of the Lord, who are before the throne of Yahweh, are our mentors and they tutor us in classrooms on the ways of the Kingdom. When the Lord asked Solomon what he wanted, he replied that he wanted wisdom. In effect, he was saying he wanted the Spirit of Wisdom and her hand maidens to be part of who he was so he could fulfil his role as king. Each of the Seven Spirits of the Lord teach us a portion of wisdom. The Spirit of Might teaches us how to operate in the counsel rooms of war; the Spirit of Wisdom has seven hand maidens and we get taught how to function in the different realms; Holy Spirit is the One who counsels and comforts and walks with us because He has taken the place of Yeshua on this earth. We can do nothing without

Him because He opens the door for us to access the other realms.

There are many Scriptures which refer to faith:

In *Mark 11:22* we read, "So Jesus answered and said to them, Have **faith in** God."

Matthew 17:20, "So Jesus said to them… because of your unbelief; for assuredly, I say to you, if you **have faith** as a mustard seed, you will say to this mountain, 'Move from here to there,' and it will move; and nothing will be impossible for you."

Ephesians 2:8, "For by grace you have been saved **through faith**, and that not of yourselves; it is the gift of God."

Hebrews 6:1, "Therefore, leaving the discussion of the elementary principles of Christ, let us go on to perfection, not laying again the foundation of repentance from dead works and **of faith** toward God."

1 Timothy 6:12, "Fight the good fight **of faith**, lay hold on eternal life, to which you were also called and have confessed the good confession in the presence of many witnesses."

1 Corinthians 13:13, "And now these three remain: **faith**, hope and love. But the greatest of these is love."

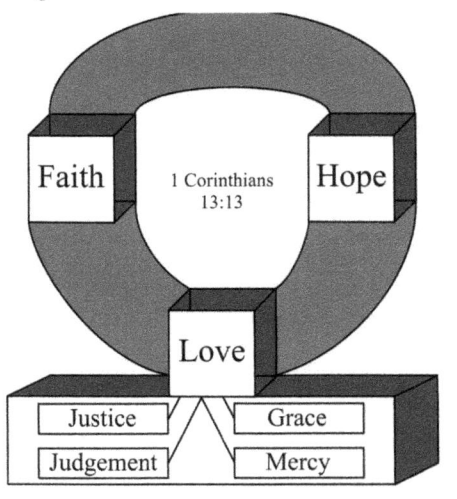

Faith | 1 Corinthians 13:13 | Hope

Love

Justice | Grace

Judgement | Mercy

Arcing of Faith/Hope/Love

The highest example of faith is found in *Hebrews 12:2*, "… looking unto Jesus, the author and finisher of our faith, who for the joy that was set before Him endured the cross, despising the shame, and has sat down at the right hand of the throne of God." Yeshua is the author or pioneer and the finisher or perfecter of our faith so that we can step into that realm and do the same thing.

Chapter 7

Full Supply

It's important to have faith and also to have a relationship with the Being of Faith because without faith it's impossible to please God. What are the things that we say and believe about ourselves? If we have anything in our flesh that is not in alignment with Yahweh as we have stepped into this 13th Tribe, within this 13th Age in Goshen, we will never reach our goal of going through the veil physically and entering into that realm. We must deal with the thoughts that we have towards ourselves on a daily basis so that we can apply faith, wisdom and knowledge in order to present ourselves as living sacrifices upon the altar. This requires us to be able to engage our soul and to place ourselves above the sun so that we stop listening to the negative chatter which lives below the sun. As we do that, we can step into the fullness of this Age of Goshen that we are in.

We must practice drinking from the **realm** of faith, not just acknowledging faith or getting to know faith. We must step in and breathe it in until the theory becomes a reality. If you need finances for something, instead of planning not to do it, rise above the sun and call the finance towards the light of your shining so that it can find you; *Isaiah 60:3*.

When Ian Clayton received the cube for the 13th Age, just before COVID, he put it into the mountain of Origin Gate. Marios Ellinas remarked that both Origin Gate and Wisdom's Echo grew exponentially; we now talk about how many Nations of the world are **not** listening to Wisdom's Echo and in fact there are about 38 Nations left that still have to join before the **entire world** is listening. Ian said this: "I feel that the altar to us is like what the Ark was to the Jews." In other words, it's the cube that will take us into this new place. Scripture says that whoever had the Ark received prosperity. If we engage in this 13th Age, by faith, the cube will begin to unlock and we will begin to prosper as we go into the land of Goshen. When things go awry in the world economically, it will not touch us. Those who are above the sun and turning towards the mountain of the 13th Tribe within Goshen, with understanding, will begin to eat and drink from this modern day Ark.

It's good to practice drinking from the well of faith because the more we do that the more we are able to let our inward light shine out. When that light is released from us, the demonic realm and the things that are hindering us or making things difficult for us will have to go. Like the widow whose oil did not run out I found that place of provision when the city I was living in was subject to massive looting because of an attempted coup in the country. The whole community came together and set up blockades to protect our suburb from being attacked and many folks gathered to do guard duty. I volunteered to make soup to feed everyone as it was winter time and quite cold. I hadn't done any grocery shopping because the shops were not open due to the looting but for a few nights I kept making bean and potato soup even though I only had two potatoes and some beans in my pantry! I then realised, that because of the need, my oil would never run dry. When I was asked how that was possible, I said that my oil will not run dry and I physically felt something come over me and cover me.

Our inland Hubs obtained travel permits and sent 3 tons of food down to us. When the goods arrived, we set up two stations in two different suburbs and started distributing food to our Hub members who also gave to people they knew. We had enough supplies to feed approximately 30 families. When the looting came to an end and businesses started operating again we were feeding about 120 families well into the next month. On one of the days, I was helping our neighbours with some supplies and they asked if I had any cooking oil. I had just given away the last bottle but when I turned around, there was a box full of oil at my feet. The same thing happened with the meat that had been sent to us by a farmer up North. It was the most difficult thing to get rid of the meat in my freezer because every time I gave some away, it would reappear.

I have a real passion for looking after the poor and needy and have started numerous kindergartens for the underprivileged where the children were fed and educated. We also fed the homeless folk in a particular part of our town on a monthly basis for about 15 years. We usually had enough food for about 60 people but every time we held our feeding scheme about double that amount would be waiting in line. Everyone would receive more than one helping before the food eventually finished. We understood the process of multiplication because we saw it happen on a regular basis.

In *2 Kings 4* we read, "A certain woman of the wives of the sons of the prophets cried out to Elisha, saying, "Your servant my husband is dead, and you know that your servant feared the Lord. And the creditor is coming to take my two sons to be his slaves." So Elisha said to her, "What shall I do for you? Tell me, what do you have in the house?" And she said, "Your maidservant has nothing in the house but a jar of oil." Then he said, "Go, borrow vessels from everywhere, from all your neighbours—empty vessels; do not gather just a few. And when you have come in, you shall shut the door behind you and your sons; then pour it into all those vessels, and set aside the full ones." So, she went from him and shut the door behind her and her sons, who brought the vessels to her; and she poured it out. Now it came to pass, when the vessels were full, that she said to her son, "Bring me another vessel." And he said to her, "There is not another vessel." So the oil ceased. Then she came and told the man of God. And he said, "Go, sell the oil and pay your debt; and you and your sons live on the rest."

The Hebrew word for 'vessels' is transliterated as *keli* and these vessels were not just random pots; they were valuable. The widow was asked to borrow many empty vessels and the word for 'borrow a few' is *ma'at* which means 'not little', in other words the vessels needed to be large and valuable ones.

Elisha then told the woman to enter her house; the word 'enter' is *bo* and means to carry something in or bring it near, and then she had to shut the door. The word 'shut' is *sagar* which means to be shut up or to be isolated, which reminds me of what happened during COVID. The word for 'door' is *dalet*, which means 'gate' or 'doors of Heaven'. Most translations say that the widow shut the door behind her and her sons but the word 'behind' is not in the Hebrew text; the word 'upon' is used instead which is *be'ad*. I remembered what I had felt when I had said that I was a widow and that my oil would not run out. The widow drank from the realm of faith, shut the door upon herself and her sons so that she was enclosed. The word for 'son' is *ben*, written with a *Beit*, and *Nun* which means 'the house of family or of seed line/to continue'. She then had to pour out the oil into the expensive vessels and the word used is *yasaq* which means 'firmly established'.

The world is saying that we're in an economic down-turn but if we can find this place of full supply then we and our seed line become firmly established. The widow filled the vessels to fullness, which is the word *mala*, and set them aside which is the word *nasa*. It also means to pull or pluck out. The widow asked her son to bring more vessels. The word for 'bring' is *nagas* which also means to 'draw near'. The son replied that the vessels were finished but in the original language it used the word *amar* which means to 'speak in a boastful manner'. He proudly told his mother that they had received every single vessel that was available. The oil that the widow was filling into the jars was not cooking oil; it was expensive anointing oil. When they had no more vessels, the oil stopped, which is written *amad*, and means it 'stayed, endured or remained' and they were able to take it with them.

When we give, we make room for more to come our way. Hoarding is diametrically opposed to the way that Yahweh operates because when we hoard we send the message that God cannot provide. When we decide to try and make a plan, we choose not to sit under this place of full supply and in fact, we are saying that we choose not to trust in faith. I have also never found a way to get out of debt which didn't include having to give. We have to give in order to receive.

Once I was on my way to the airport; there was a traffic jam and I missed my flight so I had to buy another ticket. When I arrived at my destination, a relative picked me up and started to blame the devil but I determined in my heart to give that money to the airline and bless them with it. If I let the money be 'stolen' from me, it would remain stolen but if I gave it away, I was making room for the Lord to send me more, pressed down, shaken together and running over. Three days later I received three times the amount that I had given to the airline so I phoned my relative to tell her that testimony because I wanted her to know what it's like to live in this place of full supply, in Goshen, which is above the sun. It's a marvellous realm to live in. When we position ourselves within the door of heaven, we position ourselves in the place of full supply so the story of the widow's oil is not actually a story but a realm. We position ourselves there by the words of our mouth and the intent of our heart. This place is not necessarily just for money; it's also a place of full supply for healing or for understanding the mysteries or understanding the Word. This is all about being positioned and letting that door come upon us so we can see what Yahweh is doing.

From every bit of income that I get, I give my *terumah*, I tithe (which I've done for over forty years) and I give to the poor because Scripture says that when I give to the poor, I lend to God. He gives back to me as I've given. I've found my place of full supply through giving. My vessel keeps getting filled so that I can give some more. The cycle is never-ending. I've never seen anyone, who has made a leverage trade, not have a spectacular turn-about or a breakthrough in business. Your money, which is your strength and leverage, opens up this place of full supply that sits in a conduit. The widow found this place. *Malachi 3:10-11* talks about the windows of Heaven being opened; these windows to the treasury room of Heaven do exist. If we camp in them, they will provide. In the Western world this means business, finances and getting out of debt; buying cars with cash and paying off your house. My husband and I used to visit business people who had unpaid contracts — they had provided a service but had not been paid yet. My husband would hold those invoices in his hand, present them to the Father and speak to each outstanding debt to be paid in full. The businesses who had not fulfilled their obligation paid their bill within the week until they were all up to date.

If an accusation or injustice has been brought against us we can go to the Mobile Court. In our time of need we can approach the Throne of Grace where the Beings of Grace and Mercy can arc over us and help us. In *Isaiah 60* we read, "Arise, shine; For your light has come! And the glory of the Lord is risen upon you. For behold, the darkness shall cover the earth, and deep darkness the people; but the Lord will arise over you, and His glory will be seen upon you. The Gentiles shall come to your light, and kings to the brightness of your rising. Lift up your eyes all around, and see: They all gather together, they come to you; your sons shall come from afar, and your daughters shall be nursed at your side. Then you shall see and become radiant, and your heart shall swell with joy; because the abundance of the sea shall be turned to you, the wealth of the Gentiles shall come to you. The multitude of camels shall cover your land, the dromedaries of Midian and Ephah; all those from Sheba shall come; they shall bring gold and incense, and they shall proclaim the praises of the Lord."

The *sefirot*, which sits within us, is the Way of the Tree of Life. The *yechida* burns within us and is the same fire that Moses saw in his encounter with the burning bush. The tree within us is Yeshua – there were two trees within the garden; one was Yeshua, who is the Tree of Life, and the other one was the Tree of the Knowledge of Good and Evil which was satan. The Tree of Life carries the fire. The *choshek*, or the mysteries, will cover the earth with deep darkness. This is the same darkness that surrounded Moses like a cloud and that also came over Yeshua – this darkness is not good for those who are not saved but if we are saved, then our eyes look at it from a different realm.

Wealth and abundance get attracted to us because of the fire and light within us and the camels will cover us and our land. The word 'camel' is the Hebrew letter *Gimel* and speaks of full supply. When we find ourselves in this place of full supply we can then call in jobs and better jobs, we can call in cancelled debt and inheritances to come to the light of our shining. When we landed the scroll of the 13th Age it pulled people in to the light of its shining and is also attracting the glory like the Ark did.

In *Luke 18:8,* the Lord asks a question: Will I find faith on the face of the earth? Faith is not something from the old school; we can learn to live above the sun, in the place of full supply in Goshen, and let that glory emanate from within us to attract the thing we need. When we partake of the body and blood of Yeshua during communion, we are eating the fruit of the Tree of Life and walking in the Way of the Tree of Life. It changes our DNA and everything about us.

Chapter 8
Generational Oil

Our upbringing usually determines our narrative and I determined that I would never let my children know if there were money issues. My husband and I were travelling and ministering full-time with our children so we would encourage them to trust with us so they could get their pocket money instead of telling them that we had no money. We lived by faith and knew that God would provide so we never allowed them to take on false responsibility or get involved with adult problems. I have my mom to thank for that because some of my happiest memories from my childhood were when we were in a tough financial situation. My husband on the other hand had to constantly deal with a poverty mindset because it was so ingrained in his family.

Engaging with our DNA is a great way to deal with root issues. Rejection is one of the major things that many people struggle with. Going to the Mobile Court to get the paperwork done helps and starts the process of healing so that there can be no accusation against us. However, dealing with our DNA is what brings the issue to an end. If I had known about this years ago I might not have been so involved in doing deliverance with people. Sometimes people are lazy and want someone else to cast demons out instead of dealing with the issue themselves. Scripture says in *Proverbs 26:2* that a curse without a cause has no place to land, so if we engage with our DNA issues it cannot hold onto anything. It also helps our future generations but they would still need to deal with some of their own issues. However, Free Masonry is very tenacious and hangs onto each generation, so each generation has to deal with it.

Having been involved in deliverance for decades, I used to believe that the sins of the father come down to the third and fourth generation. I've since changed my doctrine and view point because that is not the entire Scripture. When we misquote *Deuteronomy 5:9-10*, we actually create a breeding ground for the familiars to manifest. What it says is this: "For I, the Lord your God, am a jealous God, visiting the iniquity of the fathers upon the children to the third and fourth generations of those who hate Me, but showing mercy to thousands, to those who love Me and keep My commandments." It suddenly struck me that I didn't hate God and if I stopped feeding the familiars then they had no place to land for me and my future generations.

One of the ways that I like to delve into the mysteries, apart from encounters, is to look at the Word because I do love it and I enjoy finding out the meaning of words in the original Hebrew language. One of Aryeh Kaplan's books is called *Meditation and the Bible* where he discusses contemplation. He says that it has two elements to it; firstly, when you contemplate something and secondly, when you concentrate on it. We've been doing this by delving into and drinking from the realm of faith. In his book, Kaplan says that if you concentrate on something long enough it becomes contemplation which means to fully grasp the essence of a subject and to understand it. If we, in Christendom, could have learned to reason together more instead of being offended because people didn't see things in the same way, we might have had less denominations. Ricky made a comment and asked if God is all-knowing. Many people took offense at this and a debate ensued regarding this subject. God is an ever expanding horizon, an evolutionary Being, and so He is always discovering something new within Himself.

He is all-knowing but some time ago I heard a teaching by Dr. O, on the will of man, which really helped me. Man's will is so sacrosanct to God that He holds it very dearly and **chooses** not to know everything about us.

On the one hand, this offended my doctrinal belief structure but on the other hand, I realized it was a good thing. Did God know that Lucifer was going to fall? He did provide a Lamb before He created anything else in the case of any eventuality. If He knew, does that mean that there is no free will? We don't have to get upset when we converse like this because we are simply contemplating and having a conversation. In the Tanakh, the Scriptures will be in the middle of the page and all the rabbis will have their commentaries on the sides with their contemplations and points of view and will often not agree with each other. In Synagogue the rabbi teaches from Scripture as well as from the conflicting views of the commentaries, see *Isaiah 1:18.*

Kaplan goes on to say that concentration leads to a depth of understanding which comes from the spirit of Understanding speaking to us. Even higher than contemplation or concentration is probing the depth of an idea or subject, even if it's a controversial one, like: can demons be saved? We have probed this subject by looking at Scripture and other documents like the Book of Enoch and Jasher and we've discussed it until we have come to a conclusion. Can we still be friends with those that believe demons can be saved? Yes, we can, but they know that we don't prescribe to their point of view because of what we've seen in the Scriptures. There is nothing new under the sun which is why every forty years this doctrine of the restoration of the demonic realms, amongst others, resurfaces.

Once we have probed something, Wisdom starts to speak.
As Christians we are very strong on doctrine and sometimes
don't want to let something go that we've believed for decades.
Many believers say that demons were made when one third of
the angels followed Lucifer after the fall. There is no Scripture
to substantiate that belief but in our Christian walk we are not
encouraged to ask questions so we never probe our beliefs to
see if they are founded on truth.

Kaplan says this:
*Wisdom is the concept of nothingness in an idea. This is the state in
which it exists before it comes to the level where it can be grasped
by understanding. In this respect it is very much like the fountain
or spring which is the source of a river. Probing the depth of an idea
is this: the root reaches down to the source from which the fountain
or spring emanates. This source is called the depth of wisdom or the
hidden nature of wisdom.*

We cannot think on an idea with our own wisdom; we have to
know that nothing (no thing) is impossible for God. In wisdom,
there is nothing in an idea because in that place Wisdom can
begin to have input and speak to us but when we come to
this place of probing, with our own theology and ideology,
then we're just giving our point of view. We have to go to the
source of the river, we cannot just dig in the river. The Hebrew
word for fountain is *eyin* which is also the word for eye. So,
the fountain or the eye lingers on a subject and concentrates
on it deeply. The eye of the fountain is where we will find
understanding; we have to come to Yahweh within a place of
nothing and without our own doctrine.

I want to probe the idea that there is a door of full supply that I
have found. It's a place where the oil flows freely and as I come
without my theology, with nothing, I can probe what that looks

like, how it feels and where I'm going with it until I'm in the depths of the source of the spring of life. That gets me to a place of wisdom which then brings me to a place of understanding. We cannot bring our theology into this because that is not a place of nothingness. When Scripture says that nothing is impossible for God, the Jewish mindset understands the concept of nothingness and even in this place, at the source of it all, It's possible for Him as is stated in *Luke 1:37*. We cannot go to the source of the river of life and truth and hold our doctrine up in front of it at the same time. We have to let it go which is a core principle in the mystical movement.

There are dichotomies in Scripture; on the one hand we know God is everywhere and He will never leave us or forsake us, *Deuteronomy 31:8*, but on the other hand Scripture says in *Isaiah 55:6*: Seek Me while I may be found. Where did He go? In the Jewish understanding they explain that He moves towards us but because we cannot cope with the fullness of who He is, He withdraws because it's in the seeking of Him that we come to conclusions which we wouldn't have come to if He were always with us.

2 Kings 4:7 says, "Then she came and told the man of God. And he said, "Go, sell the oil and pay your debt; and you and your sons live on the rest." I now understand that this was generational, not just for her and her boys. The word 'sell' is *makar* or כְּמֹר and is written with a *Mem, Kaf* and *Resh*. The word 'pay' is *salam* or שַׁלֵּם and is written with a *Shin, Lamed* and *Mem* and the meaning is to take the chaos and bring its authority into covenantal peace or to finish something. The widow went and paid the debt. The word 'debt' is nesi or נשׁי and is written with a *Nun, Shin* and *Yod* and in this case means lender's money or extortion with interest. The widow had borrowed money from the lenders and they were threatening to take her sons. The prophet instructed her to complete the payments to the money lenders. When we get ourselves into debt, Yahweh's grace is still sufficient to finish what the creditors have done so we can clean up the mess we are in. The word for 'son' is *ben* בֵּן and is written with a *Beit* and *Nun*. The pictograph or paleo for *Nun* is a seed, so when he told the widow to go and pay off her debt so that she and her sons could live off the rest, I saw that it wasn't just for her sons; he was speaking to the seed-line in her sons. Everything we do today affects all our generations that are still to come. I realized that this was generational wealth! If we sit in the place of full supply and close the door, the *Dalet*, upon ourselves, we allow the oil of whatever it is that we are lacking, to flow over us.

The word for 'live' is *haya* חָיָ and means to sustain and to live prosperously, to live forever and to be restored. The words 'the rest' is *yatar* וְתָר and means to show excess or more than enough. This Scripture is so profound and speaks about the ability to create wealth for our future generations. I found that place of full supply when the door came upon me and after a while I realized that an unusual prosperity was resting upon my children.

Ecclesiastes 11:1 says, "Cast your bread upon the waters, for you will find it after many days." The word 'cast' is *salah* שַׁלַּח written with a *Shin, Lamed* and *Hey* which means to send or stretch out. The word 'bread' is *lehem* לָחֶם written with a *Lamed, Hey* and *Mem* and corresponds with the shew bread which was made holy and set apart in the tabernacle for only the priests to consume. This bread was placed on two golden plates, six loaves on each plate to represent the twelve tribes. What do we do when we cast our bread? We're casting or sending out the thing that is set apart to the Lord; perhaps our gifts and giving or our *terumah*, offering or giving to the poor. When we cast this, something comes back to us because it's holy. The word 'upon' is used in English but is actually *panayim* or faces so the Scripture says: Take your bread and stretch it out like something that is set apart as holy before the faces of the waters.

As a single woman, I'm responsible for two households and I also look after my elderly Father. The word for 'water' is *mayim* מַיִם written with a *Mem, Yod* and *Mem* which means the waters above and the waters below that are connected by the hand of Yahweh. Stretch out your giving as a holy offering, as you sit in the door of full supply, engaging with the faces of the mysteries of Yahweh so the hand of God can take you into the secrets of Yahweh. It's in these secrets that something begins to land on us. The word for 'many' is *rob* רֹב, written with a *Resh* and *Beit* which is also 'abundance' and the word for 'days' is *yom* which is today, yesterday, tomorrow which means it is outside of time. My generations to come will do well financially, because of what I've set in place in my seed-line because it's been secured and will be in abundance outside of this time, for generations to come.

Stretch out your seed, that thing that is holy like the sacrificial shew bread covered in gold, into the faces of the deep, and as you do that there is an abundance that is so numerous that it will hunt you down in your yesterday, today and tomorrow and it will secure you in this division in time, and time to come.

I'm determined that the masonic curses sitting in my family line will not get passed down to my future generations which is why I'm so fastidious about giving. My relatives were always in management positions in whichever company they worked for and yet have not much to show for it because of the stronghold of free masonry. I am determined to stop this for the sake of the next generations. I have now found the key to generational wealth and will teach it to anyone who wants to hear. All three of my adult children are house owners and are under the age of 40. We've also realized that if we look after the generation that came before us (our parents) this also opens up a dimension for us now.

The only commandment with a promise is: *Exodus 20:12*, "Honour your father and your mother, that your days may be long upon the land which the Lord your God is giving you." Generational wealth is not just money but it includes relationships amongst others things.

About Lindi

Lindi Masters has been in active ministry for 42 years. Her heart is to mentor the Body of Yeshua into 'Maturity being their Vav', rooted and grounded in YHVH and in His mysteries and secrets.

Lindi has a legacy of 3 incredible children who have all married Godly partners and she has 5 beautiful grandchildren.

She currently divides her time between the UK and South Africa.

SeraphCreative

Heaven's Heart for Earth

Seraph Creative is a collective of artists, writers, theologians & illustrators who desire to see the body of Christ grow into full maturity, walking in their inheritance as Sons of God on the Earth.

Sign up to our newsletter to know about future exciting releases.

Visit our website:

www.seraphcreative.org